Britain has the reputation of being the most haunted country in the world, one estimate putting its ghostly sites at ten thousand. Ghosts reflect the character and imagination of their race and times. Probe into the ghostlore of England, Wales, Scotland and Ireland and see what fantastical apparitions we encounter.

Haunted Pubs in Britain and Ireland

MARC ALEXANDER

'I know I must believe in ghosts because I am frightened of them' –
A barman at the George and Dragon, West Wycombe

SPHERE BOOKS LIMITED
London and Sydney

First published in Great Britain by
Sphere Books Ltd 1984
30-32 Gray's Inn Road,
London WC1X 8JL
Copyright © 1984 by Marc Alexander

For my mother
Louisa Mary Alexander

Set in Times

Reproduced, printed and bound in Great Britain by
Hazell Watson & Viney Limited,
Aylesbury, Bucks

Contents

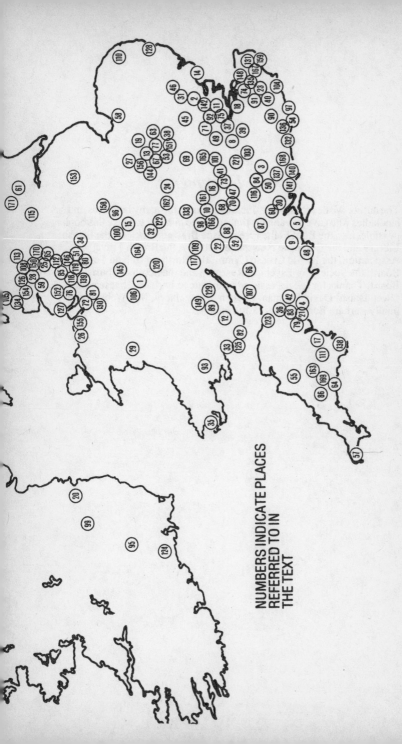

NUMBERS INDICATE PLACES
REFERRED TO IN
THE TEXT

Acknowledgements

The author wishes to express sincere thanks to the many landlords and landladies who gave up valuable time to talk to him and so make this book possible, also the Bord Failte Eireann, the Brewers' Society, the British Library and the Colindale Newspaper Library, the British Travel Association, the Bwrdd Croeso Cymru, the Northern Ireland Tourist Board, the Society for Psychical Research and the Scottish Tourist Board. Thanks for special assistance are due to Barbara Cheeseman, Owen Daish, David Dorman, Doreen Montgomery, Bob Webster and finally Barbara Boote for her skilful editing.

Introduction

Down the centuries the inns of the British Isles have provided refreshment and shelter for soldiers and fugitives, runaway lovers and persecuted priests, smugglers and highwaymen as well as millions of ordinary God-fearing travellers and – as this book will show – every type of customer has left behind ghostly impressions. As one would expect, typical pub hauntings include landlords and pretty serving wenches, robbers' victims and phantom coachmen and their vehicles – what does come as a surprise is the large number of pubs revisited by spectral monks.

The reason is that many old English inns in particular were once ecclesiastical buildings which were converted to other uses following the Dissolution of the Monasteries, others were built on the sites of such establishments and others again offered hospitality to pilgrims and clerics on journeys to religious centres.

A curious story of the persistence of a phantom priest comes from Dublin where on the corner of Summerhill and Gardner Street a pub was demolished twenty years ago. Still to be seen on the derelict site is the bottom two feet of the pub's wall which was covered with unusual tiles. Here the ghost of the priest has been seen and described as 'lamenting' for the reason that the tiles had originally graced the high altar of a church before it was demolished.

It should be remembered, too, that sometimes in the superstitious past the appearances of ghosts have been used as propaganda, and the disproportionately high number of grieving clerical spectres to be found in British ghostlore is a reflection of how many people felt about the Reformation. Cases of apparitions being given religious or political tags are

1

common, and it is interesting to note how often such ghosts belong to the losing side. Nothing lingers as romantically as a lost cause. Thus a vague wraith briefly glimpsed may have become a wronged nun, a Jacobite or Cavalier according to the taste of the day. This, of course, in no way diminishes the validity of the ghosts themselves.

Apart from conventional phantoms, pubs have a fascinating range of paranormal phenomena such as mysterious Cold Zones. An example of this was recently reported by the *Halifax Courier* in a story on the Withens Hotel which, at 1392 feet above sea level, is the highest pub in Yorkshire. The proprietor told a journalist that a century ago a traveller lost on the moors collapsed on the hotel's doorstep. He was carried inside and sat by the fire where he died of exposure, and since then the seat by the fire has always been cold.

Rarer are what may be termed 'warm manifestations' which do not relate to the actual temperature but to the amorous inclinations of ghosts. The landlady of the Whitchurch Inn near Tavistock declared that, apart from moving things about in the bar, the resident spirit gave her a 'warm hug'. And the bachelor landlord of the Old Vic in Basingstoke told the *Sunday People* in 1979 of a heavy breathing presence he sometimes experienced next to him in bed.

'It's as though there is a woman lying next to me making love,' he was reported as saying. 'She sounds a very passionate sort of woman.'

Supernatural activity is often triggered off by renovations made to ancient pub buildings almost as though ghosts do not like the environment they knew in life to be changed. There were accounts of startling happenings when a demolition team went to work on the huge Palace Hotel in Southport. Workmen reported loud disembodied voices echoing down deserted corridors, and a four-ton lift was seen on several occasions to ascend and descend by itself – after the electricity had been disconnected!

Another reason for an increase in ghostly happenings is the arrival of a new publican. It is thought that the unseen tenants are curious about him or her and try to make the newcomer aware of them. This often takes the form of poltergeist activity, and here we come to the most universal type of pub haunting.

2

In 1982 Teacher's Whisky sponsored an investigation to find the twelve most authentically haunted pubs in Britain, and seven of the final dozen were sites of poltergeist disturbance.

These mysterious entities who move objects as though by invisible hands, and who often introduce a mischievous element into their manifestations, are the most fashionable aspects of psychical phenomena today. Although their German name means literally 'noisy ghost' many investigators believe that there is nothing ghostly about them – that they are 'forces of energy' in some way related to individuals, usually children or adolescents under stress. But, as you will see over and over again in the following pages, there are accounts of poltergeist manifestations associated with pub ghosts. Also the idea of a single person being unconsciously responsible for such outbursts does not hold true because many pub poltergeists continue their dramatic and even alarming haunting after changes in landlords and staff. Those who would like to know more about this area of the paranormal should read Colin Wilson's *Poltergeist!*

Another subject you will come across in this book is exorcism. Sometimes landlords try to get rid of ghosts by calling in a priest to 'lay' them through the service of exorcism which has also received a lot of publicity in recent years. Frequently it is admitted that the pub remains haunted. According to the late Reverend Dr Donald Omand, who was a Church of England priest and one of Britain's foremost exorcists,* the object of exorcism is to relieve people and places of the influence of evil, not to oust harmless phantoms.

'I will only exorcise a spectre if it is a suffering earth-bound spirit, exerting a malign influence, or if it is a manifestation which has become a focal point for the powers of evil,' he told me.

Occasionally even something as serious as an exorcism can have a humorous side, such as when Barry Fisher, landlord of The Raven in Farndon, Cheshire, asked a vicar to exorcise the ghost of a previous landlady who was scaring the barmaids. The vicar obliged, performing the ceremony in every room in the pub except the gentlemen's toilet, with the result that this

*See *The Devil Hunter*, published by Sphere Books.

was the only place left where the poor ghost could go, and where male customers have been astonished to hear a disembodied female voice.

'It seems a bit peculiar to have a woman confined to the gents,' the landlord was quoted as saying in the *Manchester Evening News*, 'but it is a shame to rob her of the only place in the pub she's got left. I'll leave her in peace now.'

Over the ten years I have been collecting material for this book I have found that most landlords of haunted pubs do not want to drive their ghosts away. Pubs are friendly places and their phantoms are usually friendly, too, some almost being regarded as members of the family. There are even pubs which have been named after the ghosts associated with them, an example of this being The Lady in Grey in Shardlow, Derbyshire. Now a restaurant only, as a pub it was called after the ghost of a landlady who was killed there by her jealous husband two centuries ago, and who was glimpsed down the years in a grey gown.

The amount of space devoted to entries in this book varies greatly in length but each reflects the amount of information available about it. Where a haunting is particularly active or unusual, or has an interesting legend, I have written it up as fully as possible. Often pubs may only warrant a few lines because, sadly, their traditions have been lost with the passage of time. I have omitted pubs where a single manifestation relates to an individual rather than to the premises, where a ghost has been invented for purposes of publicity, or where the information available has been too meagre to hold any interest.

One reason for the loss of legends connected with pubs is that inn-keeping has largely ceased to be a family business. This loss of continuity became evident when I found that very few pubs I visited have had the same landlord over a decade and, as many have been incorporated into large chains, managers are moved from place to place with great frequency. The result is that old tales are soon forgotten. Another factor is that the traditional character 'the oldest regular' seems to have resigned his place in the snug – perhaps a victim of Space Invaders or jukebox pops – for an easy chair in front of his television set, his fund of local lore vanishing with him.

What may come as a surprise at first sight is the geographical distribution of haunted pubs. People expect Ireland and Scotland, both countries steeped in Celtic feyness, to be rich in them, yet in fact they have very few compared with England. The reason is that the inn tradition is most deeply rooted in England which, in any case, has so many more pubs – over 70,000 compared with Scotland's 4,363.

In order to avoid the boring repetition of words like 'reputed', 'alleged', 'it is said' and so on, I have written about the ghosts as if they are factual. Here disbelief is suspended, pint pots are mysteriously flung from bars, phantom coaches do roll into cobbled courtyards and White Ladies do glide along ancient passages. Whatever your view of the supernatural, remember that the pubs mentioned here are genuinely believed to be haunted by many, many people and their eerie traditions make them all the more fascinating to visit.

ENGLAND

Avon

THE GARRICK'S HEAD
(Bath. Map reference: 66)

The haunting of the Garrick's Head is a case for the connoisseur, and to appreciate its story fully we must go back to the days of Beau Nash whose house it once was. One of its rooms he used as a gambling club until 1740 when his luck at cards ran out and he lost his house to the actor David Garrick. Then half of it became the Theatre Royal where Garrick often used to appear. To save walking outside, he had a passage cut through the cellar walls so that he was able to step from his own apartments to the wings of the theatre. This private entrance to the theatre is still to be seen although it has been sealed by bricks.

'The story behind the haunting of the Garrick's Head goes back to the days when Nash had a gambling club here,' landlord Peter Welch told me. 'One day as a man was sitting at cards he discovered that his wife was having a love affair with another of the gamblers. In his fury the jealous husband stabbed the lover to death. That day the gambler's mistress was also at the club, and when she saw her husband kill her lover she rushed to the top of the house and threw herself to her death out of a window.

'Today the place is haunted by the ghosts of those two. Although I have not actually seen their shapes, I am well aware they revisit the scene of their tragedy.'

Mr Welch has a remarkably understanding approach to the presences which are very active at the Garrick's Head.

'We've done no harm to them, nor them to us,' he explained. 'We appreciate their unrest and treat them accordingly.' In fact he treats them with old world courtesy. Often when he has guests there is a mysterious knocking at the door of the dining-room. If anyone goes to the door and opens it he finds there is no one there, yet when he has resumed his place at the table the rapping starts again. At this point Mr Welch says, 'Please come in.' And there is no more knocking that evening.

'The ghost of the man seems to enjoy playing practical jokes on us sometimes,' the landlord continued. 'He hides little things, like my cuff-links for example. They disappeared from the dressing-table one day. I hunted high and low for them, but a fortnight later they were back on the dressing-table.'

Other manifestations are more dramatic.

'My wife and I were sitting in our lounge watching television one evening,' recalled Mr Welch. 'Suddenly, I saw two candles rise from their holders on the sideboard. They shot through the air, just missed my wife's head, and fell down in front of her. This was absolute fact. Candles don't normally jump into the air . . . Anyway, we left them where they had fallen until the morning.'

These are the more light-hearted aspects of the haunting, but in the room where the stabbing took place, guests who have stayed in it for longish periods – often stars who have been appearing at the Theatre Royal – have complained of a distinct feeling of unease, of being watched.

'The female ghost expresses herself in the most delightful way. Down in the cellar you get the scent of beautiful perfume, and there is no natural explanation for it at all.'

In the white-washed cellar I met the inn's odd-job man who, on his first day at the Garrick's Head, had remarked to Mr Welch, 'What's that beautiful smell down there? – I'd swear it's jasmine.'

'And jasmine it always is,' said Mr Welch.

Other people besides Mr and Mrs Welch have had vivid experiences at the Garrick's Head. In the *Western Daily Express* of 5 July 1963, a story appeared which told how the then-landlord, Bill Loud, saw the half-hundredweight cash register picked up from its place behind the bar and hurled at a chair, smashing it to pieces.

In the story the reporter, John Duller, added that two months previously he had stayed at the Garrick's Head before he had any knowledge of its reputation for being haunted.

'I can vouch for loud and mysterious bumps in the night,' he wrote. 'Several thuds woke me as I was dozing in the first floor sitting-room. I searched the room and the corridor outside for ten minutes, but I found nothing . . .'

The haunting of the Garrick's Head is not confined to the inn, but takes in the theatre next door which was once part of Nash's house. Several actors and actresses claim to have seen the Grey Lady – said to be the same phantom who favours jasmine perfume – sitting in a box above the audience.

THE NEW INN
(Backwell. Map reference: 107)

The New Inn has been troubled by the unruly ghost of an alcoholic landlady who committed suicide in the cellar. When Jim Tonkin became the landlord he told the *News of the World*, 'My wife and I are terrified. It's even worse after the bar closes. The ghost seems to stagger around, slamming doors and dropping things.'

Bedfordshire

THE GEORGE
(Silsoe. Map reference: 69)

In 1959 the readers of a publicans' trade journal were intrigued when they read an advertisement in the 'services wanted' column which required the assistance of 'a layer' to exorcise 'the Silsoe ghost'. The advertisement had been inserted by the landlady of The George who was exasperated by the activities of the inn's resident ghost known locally as the Grey Lady.

It was not that the landlady minded having a phantom on the premises, it was the tricks she got up to. These included the slamming of doors late at night and similar annoying, poltergeist-type manifestations. Members of a psychical research group heard of the advertisement and visited The George, but they failed to make contact with the mischievous spirit or to banish it.

In life the ghost who caused this consternation was a highly romantic young lady before tragedy – the puritanical of her day would say, retribution – overtook her. Her name was Lady Elizabeth Grey and she fell in love with a handsome young coachman who was based at The George. Well aware of what her father's reaction to having a commoner for a son-in-law would be, Lady Elizabeth decided to ignore convention. She and her coachman agreed to elope, and for two weeks she stayed secretly at the inn with him while her father had the neighbourhood searched for her.

After a happy fortnight with her lover, word reached her that her father had learned of her whereabouts and was heading for The George to take her home. Before he reached the inn the couple set off at high speed in a coach. Terrified of being overtaken and losing his Elizabeth, the young man whipped up his horses mercilessly. It was his undoing because the coach went so fast it careered out of control on a curve and plunged into a lake. Trapped inside, Lady Elizabeth drowned and her phantom returned to the inn where briefly she had spent the happiest time of her life.

Buckinghamshire

THE CHEQUERS INN
(Bury End. Map reference: 41)

Sad spectres from a troubled past return to this ancient
hostelry. The haunting goes back to the days when men and
women whose religious faith was at variance with that of the
current sovereign were burned at the stake – a form of
execution which was inspired by the belief that if the victim's
body was consumed by fire he or she would not be able to
receive eternal life on the Day of Resurrection.

The inn was once used as an overnight prison for seven
religious martyrs before they were led out to have the faggots
piled round them. A previous landlord quit the pub after being
kept awake night after night by groaning sounds which were
believed to have been ghostly echoes from that terrible night.
The phantom of the martyrs' gaoler has also been seen.

THE GEORGE AND DRAGON
(West Wycombe. Map reference: 73)

The village of West Wycombe comes as a pleasant surprise
after the modern sprawl of High Wycombe, a few miles to the
south-west on the A40. The village is made up of well-
preserved 17th and 18th century houses, many of them
half-timbered, which line the highway. Dominating the village
is a hill on which stands a curious circular stone structure which
is based on Constantine's Arch in Rome. It is a mausoleum
built in 1763 by Sir Francis Dashwood, the founder of the
notorious Hell Fire Club. He decorated it with friezes and
Tuscan columns and in one wall is enshrined the heart of an
18th century poet.

In the hill beneath the mausoleum are caves and tunnels

which were associated with the Hell Fire Club. There is a story that a tunnel ran from these caves to the George and Dragon which stands in the middle of the village. Its landlord, Barry James, told me of three different types of supernatural phenomena which occur regularly and are experienced by hotel staff and visitors alike.

A young barman by the name of George Campbell, newly arrived from Glasgow, frankly admitted that the hauntings made him frightened.

'I always sleep with the light on,' he said, 'and I know I must believe in ghosts because I'm frightened of them.'

The George and Dragon was built in 1720, replacing an older inn which is said to have gone back to the 14th century. It boasts a large oval sign depicting George slaying the Dragon and is probably as old as the inn. Being made of lead, it is of great weight, and is considered to be one of the most unusual inn signs in England.

In the yard, where stage coaches used to rattle in under the typical inn arch, there is still a stone for mounting horses. This old yard opens into a garden and it is here, according to legend, that the White Lady haunts on dark nights.

The first of the inn's ghosts is that of a guest who was murdered in one of the rooms upstairs. In the *Journal of the Royal Society of Arts*, published in 1933, H. Harman wrote: 'It is the age-old staircase that is supposed to be haunted . . . footsteps could be heard distinctly coming down the stairs night after night reputed to be those of a man who, by tradition, was murdered in one of the rooms in the dim past.'

Mr James said that the details of the murder had long been forgotten but added that the footsteps on the stairs continue as loud as ever.

Another manifestation concerns a poltergeist, not a vicious crockery-throwing elemental, but something with a mischievous sense of humour. Mr James explained that it makes things disappear.

'The extraordinary thing about it is that they always turn up again but never in the place where they were last seen,' he said.

He and his staff have got so used to this that they regard it as just one of the aspects of working at the George and Dragon.

While I was there he was putting up Christmas decorations in

14

the bar. At one point he went to fetch some baubles from a drawer in his desk but returned empty handed, grumbling that once again possessions had vanished – mysteriously.

The ghost for which the George and Dragon is most famous is that of the White Lady. In life she was a sixteen-year-old serving girl who worked at the George and Dragon about two hundred years ago. She was very good looking, with long golden hair, and was very aware of this and the other hotel servants referred to her mockingly as 'your ladyship'. Her name was Susan, although she seems to have been called more familiarly 'Sukie'. Three young village lads were in love with her and it amused her to play one off against the other, although she felt none of them was of the standard to which she aspired.

One day an unknown gentleman rode up to the inn. He was elegant and handsome and from his clothes he appeared to be rich. Susan was attracted immediately, no doubt contrasting his easy manners and self-confident bearing with that of her three clumsy West Wycombe swains.

She made sure that she served him and, when she took him a treacle pudding, she was so a-flutter that she put her thumb in it. Part of the crust of the pudding fell onto his breeches and with pretty confusion Sukie repaired the damage with her handkerchief. It broke the ice between them and soon the young man took to teasing the serving girl playfully. (Today whenever there is a mishap in the kitchen of the George and Dragon, such as a hole appearing in a pastry, the staff good-humouredly blame the phantom of poor Susan.)

The young gentleman came frequently to the George and Dragon to have a meal and joke with Susan. Although she did not know his name, it was rumoured that he was either a highwayman or a nobleman, the latter theory appealing most to Susan's romantic and ambitious nature. Meanwhile her three lovers watched the flirtation gloomily from the bar of the inn. Before they had been rivals, but now the presence of the unknown horseman who had so easily turned Susan's head united them in a common cause. Over their beer they planned to play a trick on Susan which, apart from humiliating her, would remind her of her station.

A message was sent to her one day purporting to come from the mysterious stranger, begging her to meet him in the chalk caves in the nearby hill the following night. It added that she was to wear a wedding gown. It may have seemed an eccentric request on the part of the young gallant, but in those days people were used to eccentricity from the 'Quality'. As she spent the day stitching a white dress, Susan doubtless envisaged herself as the romantic bride in some runaway marriage with the scion of a great family.

Next night she followed the instructions in the message and entered one of the tunnels below the Dashwood mausoleum. Instead of finding the mysterious stranger waiting for her, she saw in the light of candle lanterns the three drunken village yokels whose boorish laughter at her discomfiture echoed in the chalk cavern.

Crying with disappointment at the cruel trick which had been played on her, she picked up lumps of chalk and threw them at her tormentors. At first the three suitors continued to laugh at Susan. When several pieces of chalk had found their mark, the young men became angry and spun her round until she was dizzy. She reeled across the floor of the cave and fell, fracturing her skull against the wall. The effect of seeing her crumpled form was immediately to sober the three lads. Hoping that she had merely been stunned, they picked her up and returned to the George and Dragon.

According to one account they used the secret passage which is supposed to run between the inn and the Hell Fire Club caves. At the inn they managed to enter her room and lay her limp figure in her bed. Then they sneaked away into the night. When Susan was found in the morning she was dead.

Soon after the tragedy stories began to circulate that her spirit, clad in her pathetic white wedding dress, had been seen at the George and Dragon.

A first-hand account of the spectre was given me by Dorothy Boon, a widow whose husband had been the landlord of the inn. She continued to work there when Barry James took over, and in describing her experience she said, 'I did not realise at the moment it happened it was a ghost. I was looking for the young lady who worked in the kitchen. She was a moody little so-and-so, only about seventeen or eighteen, and I thought that something had upset her. She slept in a room in the staff quarters – the servant's room, it used to be known as – so I went to find her. I was just going by it in the passageway and looking through the window I thought, "There you are!" So I opened the door and it was just on the tip of my tongue to say, "What is the matter with you, Pat?" She was sitting on a stool looking into the fireplace, all hunched up and appearing to be very miserable. As I looked at her more closely she just disappeared!'

In the *Reader's Digest* for October 1967, the American author Jhan Robbins wrote of his experiences while staying at The George and Dragon when on his way to Oxford to work at one of the college libraries. According to his account, he went to bed and was soon asleep. Later he was awakened by a feeling of cold fingers touching his face. He pulled the cord which switches on the light and found that the sensation of fingers vanished, but when he switched off the light he again felt the cold hand. After this had happened several times he saw a pinpoint of light three feet above the floor near his bedroom door.

The light grew and he described it as having an 'opaque pearly quality'. It continued growing until it was two feet in diameter and four feet high. He switched on the light again and immediately the room was empty. As with the sensation of fingers, when he pulled the light cord to switch off the light the apparition appeared. At last he summoned up courage to get out of bed and walk towards the door where he encountered a zone of intense cold. His breathing was difficult, his limbs heavy and he asked himself if he were having a heart attack.

He added that as he stood there, feeling these sensations, he was swept by a sudden depression which, he claimed, was a sympathetic feeling towards the ghost. He felt that 'life must have felt like this to poor Sukie with no one to protect her dignity'. Then the light 'ballooned' towards him and seemed to reach him but he leapt back into bed and switched on the light – and once more the room was empty.

THE LITTLE ABBEY HOTEL
(Great Missenden. Map reference: 101)

The Little Abbey Hotel was originally built by monks of the Benedictine Order in 1151. It is, therefore, not surprising that it is thought to be haunted by the ghost of a monk. Today the hotel, a luxurious Tudor-style building standing about a mile from the Great Missenden railway station on the London road, still has traces of its ecclesiastical past. A legend lingers that it was once connected by a secret passage to Missenden Abbey about half a mile away.

According to a history available at the hotel, the Little Abbey became a convent for nuns and gained its independence from Missenden Abbey in 1188. The secret passage was believed to have been used by the monks when they came to administer the sacraments to their spiritual sisters. As there were several scandals connected with Missenden Abbey, the locals no doubt thought that the monks used the passage for more worldly purposes.

As so often happens, the pendulum swung between strictness and laxity. In 1286 it was recorded in the *Quo Warranto Rolls* that the Abbot of Missenden tried to trick one Nicholas the Taverner into signing away his inn while he lay sick in the Abbey. A canon was sent to get Nicholas' wife out of the building so that the monks could take possession of it, but, luckily for the Taverner, his wife was quick-witted. When she realised what was happening she managed to re-enter the inn by means of a ladder, and there she stayed until her husband was released and was able to lay claim to his own property.

Eleven years later, tragedy came when a young monk was found breaking Abbey rules, it is thought by committing a misdemeanour with a nun at the Little Abbey. In his short history, *Missenden Abbey*, R. H. Beevers wrote: '. . . so strict was the rule, that a certain novice was driven to cut his own throat for fear of the discipline.' It is his ghost that is believed to haunt the Little Abbey Hotel to this day.

Among the alterations and additions carried out on The Little Abbey during the past centuries is a delightful minstrels' gallery which overlooks the dining-room. It is by this gallery, in Room Number 2, that people have heard sounds which are believed to be the ghostly echoes of the monk who died by his own hand.

'This is where people say they hear peculiar things,' a senior member of the staff told me, as he ushered me into a pleasant bedroom. 'Of course you can offer explanations for most things, but I wouldn't like to say you can offer an explanation for *everything*. All I know is that the sound is loud enough to wake you straight up.'

THE OSTRICH
(Colnbrook. Map reference: 121)

The Ostrich – said to date back to 1106 – is a large rambling building with black beams framing its pink-washed walls. It is such a splendid example of a fine old English inn that an identical one was constructed in Buffalo, USA. But, though the builders at Buffalo may have got every dimension correct, the new version lacks one essential – the ghost of a murdered traveller who has haunted the inn for centuries.

The crime which led to the haunting of the inn was committed in the Middle Ages by an innkeeper named Jarman. The story is told in *Thomas of Reading* by Thomas Deloney, which was published at the end of the 17th century.

Jarman and his wife made a profitable practice of murdering solitary guests staying at the inn for the sake of their money and valuables. The method they used for killing their victims was horrific – a bed which was ingeniously contrived to drop its occupant, by the removal of a couple of bolts, into a cauldron of boiling water in the kitchen below.

The advantage of this device becomes clear when one reads the words of Deloney: 'In the dead time of night, when the victim was sound asleep, they plucked out the bolts, and down would the man fall out of his bed into the boiling cauldron, and all the cloaths that were upon him, where, being suddenly scalded and drowned, he was never able to cry or speak one word'.

The fiendish pair would remove the victim's belongings, take his horse and hide it away and then dispose of the body. Deloney wrote: 'They had a little ladder ever standing ready in

19

the kitchen, by which they presently mounted into the (bed) chamber, and there closely take away the man's apparel, as also his money, his male or capcase: and then lifting up the said falling floor which hung by the hinges, they made it fast as before. The dead body they would take presently out of the cauldron and throw it down the river, which ran near unto their house, whereby they escaped all danger.'

Twice a guest by the name of Mr Cole stayed at The Ostrich, and twice some unforeseen circumstance saved him from the Jarmans. On the third occasion he was not so lucky although, as he came to the inn, he seemed to have a sense of foreboding. To quote Deloney again: '. . . to his inn he came, and so heavy was his heart, he could eat no meat. His host and hostess, hearing he was so melancholy, came to cheer him, saying Jesus, Master Cole, what ails you tonight? Never did we see you thus sad before. Will it please you to have a quart of burnt sack?'

Mr Cole accepted their hospitality and slept soundly when he went to bed – until the agonising moment when he felt himself hurtling to his doom.

This proved to be Jarman's last murder for when he went to take Mr Cole's horse from the stable he found the door had been left accidentally open and the animal had bolted. When Mr Cole failed to return to his home in Reading, his wife dispatched servants to look for him. One found his horse wandering on the highway.

He caught the animal and led it to The Ostrich. When Jarman saw the man coming with Mr Cole's horse his guilt caused him to panic and run away. This strange behaviour aroused the suspicions of the servant who went and talked to the justices. While a hunt was organised for the innkeeper, his wife was arrested at The Ostrich and, doubtless knowing that the game would be up once the premises were searched, she confessed everything and demonstrated the falling bed to the amazed justices.

Soon afterwards her husband was captured in Windsor Forest. Just before their joint execution the couple claimed that Mr Cole had been their sixtieth victim.

Since his murder the shade of the unfortunate Mr Cole has given The Ostrich a firm reputation for being a haunted inn, although, according to landlord Derek Lamont, he has not been glimpsed recently.

In one of the inn's bathrooms Mr Lamont showed me a window which opened into the next door bedroom.

'Traditionally this is the window used by the Jarmans to make sure their victims were soundly asleep before they removed the bolts,' he explained. 'In the old days, before the bathroom was built, an outside gallery used to run along here. I feel there can be no doubt about the murders. A legend like that just can't start by itself.'

For those interested in the mechanics of the deadly bed, there is a working model in the bar. It was copied a few years ago from a much earlier one which had worn out with age and use.

Cambridgeshire

THE BLACK BULL
(Whittlesey. Map reference: 19)

Hauntings are frequently triggered off in old pubs by demolition and rebuilding. Along with the centuries-old dust and debris come ghostly visitors from the past to express their disapproval of the alterations to their old homes. This is what seems to have happened at the Black Bull twenty years ago when builders began work on the ancient structure. The ghost was said to be that of a monk who went back several centuries to when the inn had accommodated a number of holy brothers who had been involved in building a local church. It was believed in the past that he materialised occasionally on the stairs leading up to an attic, but it was the structural alterations which gave the ghost 'a new lease of life'.

THE CAXTON GIBBET
(Caxton. Map reference: 38)

The pub with this sinister name stands north of the village of Caxton, by the large roundabout where the A14 – the Ermine Street of the Romans – is intersected by the A45. There is no chance of mistaking it as on a grassy mound close by stands the stark gibbet which it is named after. Although there are no habitations close to the inn, it was a strategic site for one to have been set up as, at this intersection of roads, one of England's first toll gates was built in the 17th century. This made it an ideal place for travellers and waggoners to slake their thirst and, not infrequently, have a free spectacle of a highwayman, or some less glamorous criminal, swing into eternity.

Mrs Bishop, the wife of the landlord, said that when she and

22

her husband took over they did not know the place was haunted until a guest arrived and asked if he could stay in Room 1 as his hobby was sleeping in haunted bedrooms.

Apparently this room is haunted by a presence, a 'something' which can make the temperature drop inexplicably.

According to the story, many years ago the son of the landlord went into a room occupied by three guests who had drunk more than was good for them. One man woke up to see the young man going through his belongings. As he began to protest the landlord's son attacked him and, having killed him, slew the other two while they slept, to prevent them giving evidence against him. He then dragged the bodies to a well in the yard and dropped them out of sight.

But murder will out, and the young man was captured and hanged from the gibbet close to his father's inn.

Since then the inn has been extended and the well that was once in the yard is now beneath a trapdoor in the hallway. Apart from the coldness in the room where the murders were committed, ghostly manifestations include the sound of footsteps moving about the inn late at night, presumably those of the murderer as he dragged his victims out to the well. Mrs Bishop said that the innkeeper's son was the last prisoner to be hanged at the Caxton gallows.

From Paine and Company, the St Neots brewers who own The Caxton Gibbet, I learned more of the inn's grim history.

In the 18th century a man committed a brutal murder in Monk Field in the parish of Bourne, after which he managed to escape to America. Seven years later homesickness drove him back to England and Caxton where he had grown up. His downfall came when he had too much to drink and began to brag about his past. The result was that he was arrested and identified as a murderer by a birthmark. He was duly executed on the gallows close to the inn.

An unfortunate baker happened to be passing and noticed the hanged man was showing signs of life, the noose not having tightened sufficiently to completely suffocate him. The kindly man took pity on the victim and, having cut him down, tried to revive him by giving him some of his bread to chew. For this Christian act the baker was the next to swing from the gibbet.

Another local publican's son also ended his days above the

mound close to the inn. In 1753 he was hanged there for taking part in a mail robbery. For five months his body dangled from the arms of the gallows as a warning to others. Finally, it was blown down in a high wind. A Mr Lird, a fellow of Trinity College, Cambridge, is said to have examined the body, opening the clothes to see what state it was in. He is recorded as finding it 'dry and not offensive'.

THE CROWN INN
(Great Staughton. Map reference: 53)

From time to time manifestations at the Crown Inn have provided classic examples of a certain type of pub haunting – a haunting in which the haunter seems to take enjoyment in playing tricks on the publican and his staff. A modern view of the poltergeist is that it is not a ghost at all but some 'elemental' which focuses on an individual from whom it draws the energy to create physical disturbances. Yet in many pub hauntings poltergeist phenomena are associated with a genuine old fashioned ghost, and they are not necessarily focussed on one person as this type of haunting can go on over the years without being affected by changes of landlords and staff.

Such is the case at the Crown Inn. Local tradition associates its paranormal manifestations with a past proprietor who died while his wife was pregnant. And this activity usually takes place when a new landlord moves in, a not uncommon circumstance in haunted pubs. Certainly there was a flare up of activity a dozen years ago when a new licensee took over. He and his wife had a period of being teased by the resident entity when unseen hands knocked bottles together after the bar had been closed for the night, music blared from a radio after switching itself on and objects, especially articles of clothing, would vanish inexplicably only to appear in a different place days later.

Perhaps the most significant action by the ghost was when the landlady remarked to a customer in the bar that she did not believe in the supernatural. No sooner were the words out of her mouth than a clock above the bar appeared to leap off the wall.

24

THE FERRY BOAT INN
(Holywell. Map reference: 63)

The White Lady, who haunts the Ferry Boat Inn in the very heart of the legend-ridden fenland, is probably the longest established ghost to glide mysteriously in any English hostelry. Yet the fascination of her tragic story has not diminished during the last ten centuries. A few years ago over 400 people congregated on the anniversary of her death in the hope of seeing her wraith rise from an old tombstone set in the floor of the inn's bar.

In the low-ceilinged bar of the inn – which, according to *The Guinness Book of Records*, claims to be the oldest in England – I learned about the haunting from burly Tom Arnold. He is a well-known countryman and an expert on the fenland craft of rush cutting. He has lived most of his life next door to the Ferry Boat Inn.

'I'd always known about the legend, but it was about twenty year ago that we found out more about it,' he said. 'At that time there was a lot of fuss about the Loch Ness monster. The landlord, who had just taken over the Ferry, said he wished there was something like that here because it would be good for business.

' "Why," I said, "you've got the White Lady right here on your premises." And I told him about the ghost which is supposed to be seen once a year on 17 March – Saint Patrick's Day – in the bar. Well, he got very interested in the tale and, to cut a long story short, psychic research people and clairvoyants were invited here. One claimed to have made contact and to have gained the full story of the ghost. They even got to know her name – Juliet Tewsley.'

Juliet Tewsley was born in Holywell during the reign of King Edward the Confessor. Probably little of what went on in the outside world reached the village in the heart of the fenland. Perhaps a pedlar would bring word of the great abbey the King was building in distant London – or news of the troubles with the Northmen would come with the boats which sailed up the River Ouse, steering for a beacon light on the top of the church tower when fog cloaked the marshes. Yet Holywell must have been a microcosm of the outside world, and the happenings in the next village as interesting to Juliet as news from Normandy was to a Londoner.

As she grew up Juliet became what would be described today as 'temperamental'. She was passionate and strong willed, yet given to fits of depression such as many young people pass through while growing up. No doubt many heads shook in Holywell when she fell madly in love with Tom Zoul. He was a local woodcutter and the village tearaway who enjoyed nothing better than carousing with other lads of Holywell and the surrounding villages. Although Tom returned Juliet's love, he was not as serious as she and did not want to spend all his free time with her.

Tragedy came one St Patrick's Day when Tom Zoul went off drinking with some village lads and Juliet wandered disconsolately by the river. The more she brooded on Tom's having a good time while she suffered from his absence, the more depressed she became. Surely, if he preferred the company of young men to hers, it could only mean he did not love her. At Juliet's age it was easy to change from happiness to despair and, while in this latter mood, she committed suicide.

Tom Zoul found her body swinging from the branch of a tree by the river's edge, close to where the ferry boat made its crossings during the day.

As Juliet had taken her own life, the local priest could not allow her body to be buried in the churchyard. According to custom she was laid to rest at the crossroads, in this case the crossroads at the bank of the river close to where she had hanged herself.

A stone slab marked the grave and that, apart from the remorse in Tom Zoul's heart, should have been the end of the story. But when the Ferry Boat Inn was built over the spot, Juliet's tombstone was incorporated into the stone floor of the bar, and her restless spirit has returned to it again and again throughout the passing centuries. The stone has remained as part of the flooring to this day, having been trod by countless generations of inn customers.

'Once it was removed and the earth underneath dug through a couple of feet,' Tom Arnold said. 'There used to be a story that there was treasure under it, but I reckon if they had dug deeper they would have found Juliet's bones.'

The white wraith of the girl has been seen to materialise above the stone and then float away in the direction of the river. This manifestation is rare, but there is no shortage of reports of odd happenings in the inn such as strange sounds and the mysterious opening and closing of doors. Tom himself has not seen the apparition but, like many others, he has had the experience of a locked door unaccountably opening late at night. Dogs do not like the bar and some growl and bristle with fear when they are taken close to the slab.

While I was in the bar a lady told me how she and several of her friends had experienced one of the commonest super-natural manifestations at the Ferry Boat Inn. In the bar one day, they were suddenly aware of mysterious music that seemed to come from nowhere. It was 'old fashioned and very beautiful'. This unearthly dirge for poor Juliet is one of the best known features of the Ferry Boat's haunting and, strangely enough, can only be heard by women.

THE GOLDEN LION
(St Ives. Map reference: 77)

The fact that Oliver Cromwell took up a farm near St Ives in 1630 is commemorated in the town's market place by a rather fine statue of the Protector in a very unpuritanical hat. It was erected at the beginning of this century, and was originally destined for Huntingdon, where Cromwell was born. The citizens there refused to have it, so St Ives gained its famous statue.

Opposite is the Golden Lion which dates back to the 16th century. It used to be a coaching inn, but now the yard into which the coaches used to rumble has been roofed over to make a large lounge. The balconies, on to which the luggage was unloaded from the tops of the vehicles, still remain to connect the hotel's bedrooms.

It used to be believed that on the thirteenth night of each month Cromwell's spectre walked along one of these balconies to a room in which he once stayed. But, when I visited the inn, I learned that the ghost which gives the Golden Lion its most deserved reputation for being haunted is the Green Lady.

Landlord Douglas Seymour said that many residents in the hotel had vowed that their belongings had been mysteriously moved about in their rooms. He added that no one knew who the Green Lady was, or why she should haunt the inn, although one vague legend suggests she might have been Cromwell's mistress.

When Mr and Mrs Seymour took over the Golden Lion they found in Room 14 – the haunted room – a picture of a lady to which they attributed supernatural disturbances, and when they removed it the manifestations lessened. The picture certainly did not date from Cromwellian times, it looked more like one of those rather brightly coloured pictures popular in Victorian days. Its effect was like that of a tinted photograph.

Signed by Herbert Herkomer, it depicted the face of a striking-looking woman with vine leaves in her hair who appeared to be gazing mysteriously into the middle distance. Whether this picture was a copy of an earlier painting of the Green Lady, or whether it had some other mysterious connection with the haunting, no one can tell today. Yet the fact remains that the combination of the picture with Room 14 has caused many people to experience psychic phenomena.

At the inn I met Mike Samuels who told me that he had been staying in Room 14 when he woke up in the night as the bed clothes were whipped from his bed.

'I saw nothing,' he said, 'but the door opened and closed by itself, as though someone invisible had passed through. I cannot say I was frightened – in fact the unusual experience left me with a rather pleasant feeling.'

THE SPREAD EAGLE
(Croxton. Map reference: 151)

There is a morbid link between the Caxton Gibbet (see page 22) and the Spread Eagle. This village pub stands close to what is believed to have been a burial ground for felons hanged at the Caxton Gibbet three miles east on the A45. In the days of public execution a hanging was always an excuse for a vast intake of ale and spirits by the spectators, and no doubt when they followed the cortège to witness the victim's remains interred in unhallowed ground the access to a second pub was very welcome.

There is a tradition that the ghosts of those who died at the Caxton Gibbet haunted the Spread Eagle. This could account for the aural manifestations which have troubled some past landlords. This activity appeared to reach its height a few years ago when Arthur Hawe was the licensee.

He described the noise he and his wife heard late at night as sounding as though the bar was full of customers, talking and walking about. When he went to the bar it was always empty and the pub securely locked up. Perhaps even worse than the unseen revelry was a ghastly rasping sound as though someone was having difficulty in breathing . . .

When the Hawes first moved in they could not sleep for the sounds, although they gradually got used to life in a haunted pub. Perhaps it was a mercy that the phenomena were only aural – one does not like to think of what might have been seen if the ghosts had been visible.

Cheshire

THE GEORGE AND DRAGON
(Chester. Map reference: 72)

The pub which has one of the most ancient hauntings in Britain is itself less than fifty years old, but the fact that it stands on a Roman burial ground may have something to do with it. The manifestation which, if it is Roman, must go back at least sixteen centuries, takes the form of heavy disembodied footsteps marching through the pub – walls and all. After an interval of some minutes, the sounds are heard again but this time they appear to approach from the other end of the building. Remembering that the George and Dragon stands in the Roman city of Chester, it does not take a great effort to imagine a legionary on sentry duty.

HARRINGTON ARMS
(Gawsworth. Map reference: 80)

It would seem that this pub shares a beautiful phantom with nearby Gawsworth Hall. The hall is well known for its supernatural manifestations – twelve years ago the air close to a secret room used for hiding priests during the days of religious persecution was filled with the smell of incense. But its most famous ghost – 'a lady in ancient costume' – is believed to be that of Mary Fitton who was a Maid of Honour at the court of Elizabeth I.

Gawsworth Hall was Mary's family home, but it was in London that her beauty and charm made her famous and sought-after. There is a theory that she was the Dark Lady of Shakespeare's sonnets. When she had been in the Queen's service for six years it was reported to Her Majesty by Sir Robert Cecil that she was pregnant. Elizabeth was furious, perhaps through jealousy – the queen had referred to herself bitterly as 'a barren stock' when news reached her that Mary Queen of Scots was with child. For her 'effrontery' Mary Fitton was imprisoned in the Tower of London. Also imprisoned was the Earl of Pembroke for his part in the scandal. Mary finally married Captain William Polewhele by whom she had first had an illegitimate son.

In Elizabethan times there was a farmhouse where the Harrington Arms now stands, and perhaps strolling to it had been a favourite occupation of young Mary before she left home and was caught up in the intrigue of the court. This could be an explanation for the evening journey made from time to time by her ghost down an avenue of trees from the hall to the door of the pub where she melts away.

THE HEADLESS WOMAN
(Near Duddon. Map reference: 81)

An inn which takes its name from a ghost is the Headless Woman which stands on the road between Tarporley and Duddon in Cheshire. In the bar, where the old black beams gleam with copper and brass ornaments, the landlord's wife, Heather Blythe, showed me a small statue of a woman standing with her head beneath her arm.

'This is a replica of a large carving which used to stand outside the pub,' she explained. 'Unfortunately, it was stolen some time ago. My husband and I have not seen the headless ghost, but the landlady before us swore that she had seen it. It's a well-known spook in this neighbourhood.'

'Our predecessor experienced it twice,' said Arthur Blythe. 'It was written up in the newspapers at the time. The ghost is supposed to come along the old bridle path from Hockenhull Hall which comes out on to the Tarporley road close to this place.'

The story goes back to the Civil War when the Parliamentarians were marching across Cheshire. The Royalist family who lived in Hockenhull Hall at the time collected their silver and buried it secretly in the grounds. Then they fled, leaving an elderly servant in charge of the estate, thinking her advanced

31

years would safeguard her against any ill-treatment.

When the troops arrived they had already heard of the Hockenhull treasure and they were eager to loot it. As they broke into the Hall, their anticipation turned to fury when they saw that all the valuables had been removed. When the servant refused to reveal the hiding place, they began to torture her. Throughout the ordeal the old woman remained steadfast to her trust, and when she finally found release in unconsciousness, one of the men struck her head from her body with his sword.

THE ROYAL GEORGE
(Knutsford. Map reference: 139)

The traditional ghost of the Royal George is that of a highwayman named Edward Higgins who led a double life before his long career of crime ended on the gallows. By day he played the role of a fashionable man-about-Knutsford, by night he was a daring road agent. One history of the town states that he hunted with the gentry in the morning, dined with them in the afternoon, and robbed them after nightfall.

Often he would frequent the Royal George in order to see who would be worth holding up on their way home. One evening at an assembly there he was dazzled by the jewels worn by a certain Lady Warburton. He left early and took the Arley road to a point among some dark trees which made an ideal place for his ambuscade.

When he heard the rumble of her carriage wheels he spurred forward ready to deliver the highwayman's command. Just at that moment the moon came from behind the clouds and Lady Warburton recognised the horseman outside her window.

'Goodnight, Mr Higgins,' she cried. 'How naughty of you to leave so early.'

The result was that Mr Higgins had to escort her home like a dutiful cavalier, no doubt fighting to retain his self-control when he saw her ladyship's diamonds glittering in the moonlight.

Suspicion was finally aroused against him when early one morning he was seen leading his horse to its stable – in order to deaden the sound of its hoofs he had used the old highwayman's trick of putting woollen stockings over them.

Cornwall

THE DOLPHIN
(Penzance. Map reference: 57)

The Dolphin is a smallish, grey building standing on The Quay at Penzance, close to where the *Scillonian* berths after its regular voyage from the Scilly Isles. It faces a scene of nautical bric-a-brac, such as mounds of rusting chains and great red buoys which look like models for a Wadsworth painting. The origins of it as a waterside tavern are lost in history, but there is a very strong local legend that Hawkins briefed his captains under its low ceilings before the battle with the Invincible Armada. It is also believed that the first pipeful of tobacco to be smoked in England was enjoyed there by Sir Walter Raleigh. This is quite likely as it is recorded that Ralph Lane, the first Governor of Virginia, brought tobacco and smoking implements for Raleigh in 1586, and it was usual for ships from America to make their English landfall at Mount's Bay to take on fresh water and supplies at Penzance before continuing to their home ports.

Brian Clark and his wife Mary had only been running the inn for six months when I visited it, but in those six months they had found that the stories about The Dolphin being haunted were perfectly true.

'We know The Dolphin is one of Cornwall's oldest taverns, and there is no doubt it was used by smugglers,' said Mr Clark.

Some time ago, when repairs were being carried out in the cellars, a small smugglers' hiding place was discovered. In it were two casks still in good condition from the days of the freetraders.

At the turn of the century, The Dolphin changed from being a sailors' tavern to a hotel of great respectability. In those days it had become fashionable for the gentry to visit the Scillies for holidays, and they stayed at The Dolphin while awaiting the packet. There is still a small waiting room where the ladies retired while their menfolk downed brandies and grogs in the male precincts of the bar.

Now The Dolphin has regained its old tavern atmosphere, yet through its changes its ghost has remained constant, an old seadog known locally as George. How far back he dates or what his history was no one knows, but there is no doubt that he makes his presence felt. A regular told me how the previous landlady frequently saw him, and Brian and Mary Clark swore they had heard him recently.

'It was very early one morning,' Mr Clark explained. 'We had set the alarm for five o'clock because we had guests here as a result of a cancellation in the helicopter service to the Scillies. As they were getting up early to cross by ship we had to get up extra early to prepare breakfast.

'As I was lying in bed – my wife had already got up – I heard a heavy tramp, tramp, tramp of someone marching along the corridor and going down the stairs. There was no doubt at all that it was the heavy tread of someone walking on wooden floorboards. After a short while I heard whoever it was coming back, up the stairs and along the corridor past our room. As I lay there I thought it was a guest walking about, until I realised it could not have been – the stairs and the corridor are carpeted!'

In another part of the building Mary Clark heard the mysterious footsteps. Tactfully she questioned the Dolphin guests at breakfast – not one of them had been out of bed when she and her husband heard them.

The Dolphin's chambermaid knew more about the old sea captain. She said that in Room 4 there was often a mysterious depression in the cushion of a certain chair. The cushion could be shaken up and replaced and, even though the room was shut up and not used, the indentation always reappeared. In Room 5 next door the signs were more spectacular. There was often an indentation in the bed and on the pillow as though someone had slept in it.

'Not long ago, two elderly maiden ladies stayed in Room 5,' the chambermaid said. 'When I went in to clean out, I was surprised to find tobacco ash scattered about the floor. It struck me as strange that two such nice old ladies should not bother to use the ashtrays, and what was even stranger was that they should use coarse pipe tobacco, the old fashioned sort in long strips.

'When they left the room remained vacant, but after a couple of days I went in to dust and make sure everything was all right. And there – just as it had been when the two ladies were there – was a scattering of tobacco. It was as though somebody had knocked out their pipe so that tobacco and ash went everywhere. Well, at least I know enough now not to blame the old ladies.'

Soon after the Clarks took over The Dolphin they became aware of another ghostly presence.

'I saw him twice in one week,' said Mary. 'For some days before, my husband and I and our small son had been strangely restless. I do not know how to describe the feeling, but it was a very unusual one for us. Then one night, in the early hours really, I woke up and saw a figure standing at the foot of the bed. It was a young man with fair hair. At first I was terrified as I thought someone had broken in, and I remember wondering why the front door had not been barred properly. Then I felt my fear leave me, and as I did so the figure just melted away.'

THE FINNYGOOK INN
(Crafthole. Map reference: 64)

This pub is one of the select few whose names are inspired by their ghosts. Just over thirty years ago its name was changed from the New Inn to the Finnygook Inn in honour of the smuggler whose ghost made its presence felt there. His name was Finny and he led a gang of 'freetraders' who operated in the Whitsand Bay area. The old New Inn was their favourite meeting place and it was here that excisemen came upon them as they were preparing to take a load of contraband to Plymouth. Shots were exchanged and as the smugglers retreated their leader was left lying dead.

From then on his gook – a Cornish word for a phantom – returned to the inn where he was said to be responsible for eldritch noises and the sometimes playful paranormal activity which is usually attributed to poltergeists. Strangely, since the inn was named after Finny's ghost his visits there ceased. Perhaps this is one way of 'buying off' a ghost – landlords of haunted pubs please note.

JAMAICA INN
(Bolventor. Map reference: 86)

The slate-grey bulk of Jamaica Inn – made famous by Daphne du Maurier's novel – is in keeping with the wild moorland it overlooks. Bodmin Moor has always been a strange and lonely place which all but the most stout-hearted tended to avoid. And it was not just the fear of smugglers or highwaymen – even today there is something brooding, hostile and 'other-worldly' about it. A few miles from Jamaica Inn is a stretch of water known as Dozmary Pool where according to legend the sword Excalibur was returned to the Lady of the Lake by command of the dying King Arthur.

The Jamaica Inn owes its present existence to a road which was made across the moor following the 1769 Turnpike Act. It became a place to change horses on the Truro-Launceston route and, according to Murray's *Handbook for Travellers*, published in 1859, the inn was 'frequented by sportsmen in the winter and affords comfortable though somewhat rude accommodation'. But it was not just sportsmen who frequented Jamaica Inn. Before the coach road was built it was connected to the outside world only by a rutted track and this isolation made it an ideal spot for the activities of smugglers who brought their contraband here from the coast under the cover of darkness. It was then collected by waggons and distributed as legitimate merchandise to various cities in southern England including London.

It is only to be expected that such an inn should be haunted. The story of the resident phantom is that he arrived late one afternoon and ordered a meal. It is thought that he was a seaman who had been paid off in Falmouth, and would therefore be likely to be carrying a substantial sum of money – another version of the legend makes him a pedlar with a valuable pack of goods.

While waiting for his meal he sat outside, a tankard of ale in his hand, unaware that he had caught the attention of some of the footpads who infested Bodmin Moor in those days. The sun was setting when the landlord called him in to eat, but when he was halfway through his supper one of the thieves managed to lure him outside on some forgotten pretext. He did not return and those in the inn knew better than to go searching for him in the dark.

In the morning the traveller's corpse was found in the yard, his pockets empty. Since then his grey spectre has been seen from time to time, sitting on the stone wall which surrounds the yard in front of the inn, just as he did that afternoon long ago when he enjoyed his ale after a long trek over the moor.

Derbyshire

THE CASTLE HOTEL
(Castleton. Map reference: 34)

At the Castle Hotel the finishing touches were being put to the tables which were laid for a lavish wedding breakfast. The flower arrangements did not have a leaf out of place, on the top table silver tokens gleamed on the large white wedding cake waiting for its ritual slicing and wine waiters hovered, ready to start pouring drinks the moment the laughing guests should arrive. In a nearby church the mother of the bride dabbed a handkerchief to her eyes while her husband glanced anxiously at his watch. Outside the best man looked up and down for a sight of the bridegroom, conscious that the bride's carriage had arrived and she was waiting in it . . .

As things turned out the flowers in the Castle Hotel were never admired, the cake remained uncut and the wine waiters regretfully returned the bottles to the cellar. Word had come by a harassed-looking messenger to cancel the reception – the groom had not turned up for the ceremony.

The jilted bride never properly recovered from the shock, and although it happened long ago, her white veiled phantom has returned on many occasions to the Castle Hotel, sadly revisiting the spot where she had once hoped to be toasted at her wedding breakfast. Each time this sad spectre has been seen it was in the passage which leads to the hotel dining-room.

THE MALT SHOVEL
(Shardlow. Map reference: 96)

Alone in the pub which was being renovated, the builders' apprentice whistled as he carried some timber up a flight of stairs. Reaching the top he put down his load and then his whistling was replaced by a cry of alarm. An invisible force suddenly pressed against him, bearing him backwards despite his frenzied struggles. It would have been bad enough to be propelled towards the edge of the stairs by a flesh-and-blood adversary, but when the enemy could not be seen it was a horrifying situation.

Inexorably the youth felt himself being pushed towards the brink, his heels slid over the edge of the top step and next instant he was tumbling down the stairs.

Luckily he was only bruised, and when he told his workmates about his experience they laughed at him, thinking he was embroidering an accident in which his foot had merely slipped. They laughed, that is, until their boss lurched into the bar, his face grey with shock. While the landlord poured him a stiff drink, he muttered how an invisible 'thing' had thrown him downstairs.

It was then that talk of Humphrey began, a vindictive ghost who had obviously been raised by the alterations being carried out in the pub.

The Malt Shovel, which stands on the Trent and Mersey Canal, was built at the end of the 18th century as a house for the manager of the next-door malt-house, hence the name given to it when it was changed into a pub. According to local legend an early foreman drowned a tramp in a vat in the maltings, and it was his ghost – known as Humphrey – which remained earthbound at the canalside pub.

Apart from his attacks on the apprentice and the builder, Humphrey's most spectacular manifestation was one night when he burst open a bricked-up doorway, scattering the bricks outwards over the floor. When the reconstruction of the Malt Shovel's interior was completed, the frightening phenomena ceased to the relief of the landlord, and since then the pub has remained a quiet house, at least as far as the supernatural is concerned.

Devon

THE BISHOP LACY INN
(Chudleigh. Map reference: 17)

Strange things began to happen at the Bishop Lacy Inn when Melvin Bannister took over in August 1982, but he was hardly surprised – he had known of its reputation for being haunted before he arrived.

'It's interesting the number of people who have seen the ghost in the past and who don't really want to see it again . . . just the one occasion and usually they have not been on their own at the time,' he told me. 'Certainly a lot of people in the village believe in it and some are scared to come upstairs. Personally, I believe the ghost is very friendly.'

The phantom associated with the inn is that of Bishop Edmund Lacy of Exeter. In the 14th century the building, which was later named after him, was his summer residence.

'You can see where there used to be a chapel upstairs,' Mr Bannister said. 'The beams go up in an apex which was the chapel ceiling. I believe the inn was the only building not to be burned down in Chudleigh's fire in 1807. The lounge with its beams is original, and there's a door which opens into a tunnel which is believed to come out somewhere near the church. Unfortunately I have not been able to explore it because it has caved in beneath the road.'

When I spoke to Mr Bannister he had not seen the phantom which, with its old fashioned black cloak, would not be easy to mistake.

'But when I moved in the ghost – or whatever it was – looked me over to see if I would do,' he explained. 'Apparently it was satisfied because the haunting only lasted a month. It expressed itself in strange ways but nothing was ever moved or thrown about like it would have been with a poltergeist. A lot of the activity had to do with electrical things. One example I remember well was when an electric kettle started to heat up by itself. It wasn't even switched on yet it began to boil.

'On another occasion my sister came down for a weekend with her husband. On the first day she went to make a cup of tea – and the water tap turned itself on before her eyes. The result was that she walked out.'

THE BLACK DOG HOTEL
(Uplyme. Map reference: 21)

A popular figure in English ghostlore is the phantom hound. Some folklorists believe that it was 'imported' by the Norse settlers who came to Britain before the Norman Conquest, the legends being inspired by their belief in Odin's terrifying War Hound. Although the phantom hound has a variety of names, the fundamental belief in him was widespread in England. He is known as the Barquest in Northern England, in Anglia he is Black Shuck, and in other areas he has been feared as Padfoot, Shriker, the Galley Trot and the Shug Monkey.

I think the most eerie of all the supernatural animals are the coal-black Yeth Hounds – also known as the Wish Hounds – who begin their wild hunt from Wistman's Wood in the heart of Dartmoor for the souls of unbaptised children, or so says one tradition which has a certain propaganda ring about it. Some believe that the Yeth Hounds provided the inspiration for Sir Arthur Conan Doyle's novel, *The Hound of the Baskervilles*.

Spectral hounds have also been responsible for the naming of some English pubs, which brings us to the Black Dog Hotel in Uplyme which appears to be perched on the Devon–Dorset border. According to an article in the *Bridport News* the inn took its name from a ghostly dog which used to haunt a partly demolished mansion next door where it had been responsible for the owner finding a hoard of coins from the reign of Charles I. Since then it has been said to materialise in the lanes in the vicinity, especially Black Dog Lane which runs past the hotel's back garden.

'There are various stories about the haunting but the one which seems to be the most popular in Uplyme is that a previous owner of the pub had a lot of money stored in his attic,' Mrs Raffo of the Black Dog told me. 'This caused someone to break in and murder the landlord. His dog was also killed trying to protect his master. Consequently he is supposed to haunt the Black Dog. I have never seen him, but we haven't been here for very long. Some locals say that he is still seen outside in the lane.'

THE DEVIL'S STONE INN
(Shebbear. Map reference: 55)

It is very unusual for the Devil to be named on an inn sign, but in the case of the Devil's Stone Inn it is inspired by a unique piece of English folklore. Every year on November 5 the ringing of the church bell summons the villagers to overturn a large stone, known as the Devil's Boulder, which lies under an oak tree in the square. For centuries it has been the traditional belief that peace and prosperity for the village will be ensured if this stone is turned over annually and, according to the local vicar, it is a ceremony that is likely to continue into the far future.

The haunting of the Devil's Stone Inn is the result of a murder which was committed at the pub.

'Many years ago a man and his seven-year-old daughter arrived at the inn late at night,' said owner Robert Rimmer. 'They were fleeing from someone – or something – and the father was killed at the inn. The ghost is the young girl, possibly looking for her father.'

The ghost is most likely to be seen by children who have described her as wearing a knee-length white smock. A farming student named Bruce Wingrave-Pain told the press in 1982 how he had seen the resident phantom.

'I was in one of the hotel bedrooms talking to a friend when I saw the girl with a grey-bearded man,' he said. 'She was sitting in the corner with her hands covering her face . . . but she's friendly and I don't feel frightened.'

In an investigation into British haunted pubs sponsored by Teacher's, the Devil's Stone Inn was among the twelve selected as the most interesting.

THE HARE AND HOUNDS
(Honiton Common. Map reference: 79)

One of the gipsy ghosts to find his way into this book appears at Christmas time when he walks across the common to the Hare and Hounds. Although he is well known in the neighbourhood – where it is believed his annual walk is in search of a seasonal pint – his origins have been long forgotten.

On Christmas Eve fourteen years ago he was seen by a young couple half way across Honiton Common. Dusk was just falling when they saw a tall gipsy-looking man walking towards them, and they might have regarded him as an ordinary wayfarer had he not been wearing clothing which would have looked in place a century ago, and old-fashioned leather leggings. But what aligned with local belief was his headgear – a hat with a broad brim rolled up at the sides of a 'most beautiful pale green', a colour which has always been associated with the fairy folk who were once so populous in the West Country.

THE OLD INN
(Widecombe-in-the-Moor. Map reference: 111)

The Old Inn has stood in the Dartmoor village made famous by the traditional song 'Widecombe Fair' for six centuries. According to villagers it is haunted by the spectre of a man, usually seen in the afternoon, walking from the inn's kitchen into a smaller room. He appears quite solid until he fades like a figure in an un-fixed negative when it is exposed to the light.

The other supernatural phenomenon is the sound of a child crying piteously in one of the upstairs bedrooms. Only newcomers bother to investigate – they soon learn that when they enter the room in response to the sobs, there is nothing for mortal eyes to see.

The story behind the fading man and the crying child is another of those where the events which triggered off the haunting have been long forgotten. Nevertheless, the hauntings continue regularly.

'I have heard the sound of crying all right,' said landlord Geoffrey Ellis. 'Although I have not seen the figure of the man appear in the kitchen myself, there is no doubt that my wife has.'

If you travel north from the village for about two miles – until you are close to the Hound Tor Inn – you will find an old grave mound with a weathered headstone near the narrow road. This is known locally as Jay's Grave, and is the resting place of Mary Jay who was buried in unhallowed ground over a century ago.

She was a poor workhouse apprentice who hanged herself after she had been deserted by her lover. It is a sad little monument to the age-old theme of trusting love and selfishness. The odd thing is that, after all this time, her grave is never without flowers. To quote *Dartmoor Discoveries*, a small guidebook which is on sale at Widecombe: 'Nobody has been able to discover who places them on the mound. The mystery remains in spite of a watch being kept to discover the secret.'

THE ROYAL CASTLE HOTEL
(Dartmouth. Map reference: 138)

It is to be expected that phantom coaches are associated with inns, but the Royal Castle Hotel is unique in that it is the only one where a ghostly vehicle is heard to rumble right through the building itself. To find out about this phenomenon I visited the hotel, which began as a tavern in 1587, and heard the story from Gwyneth Powell, the proprietress.

'The first time I heard the noise of the coach was twenty years ago, though at the time I did not realise what it was,' she said. 'My husband was seriously ill and in a delirium. I was nursing him and it was very late, perhaps two o'clock in the morning. Suddenly I was aware of a dull rumble coming from below. It seemed to start some distance away and then get louder and louder. I vaguely thought someone might be rolling an empty barrel, but because of my husband's condition I did not give it much thought. But from his bed he said, "There's Queen Mary's carriage just arrived . . . can't you hear the horses? I don't suppose the receptionist has told her the coach is ready."

'As he spoke it did occur to me that the sound was rather like horses and the noise that iron-bound wooden wheels would make on cobbles, but, as I said, I took little notice because I was so concerned for my husband who was dying.'

Two years later Mrs Powell heard it again at the same time as before – two o'clock in the morning.

'The noise woke me up,' she said. 'At first I thought that someone was rolling beer barrels about outside. Although I was very sleepy, I got up and went to the window, but there was nothing to be seen. And suddenly I realised I had been thinking of horses' hooves as I had opened my eyes. That's what we hear first, the sound of an outrider galloping in. It is followed by the noise of the coach, the opening and closing of its doors and then the rumble of its wheels as it moves off again.'

This phenomenon has continued for many years, not always on the same date but always at the same time. The earliest it has been heard in any year is 12 September, and the latest in November.

'During that period it is not unusual for guests to say to me, "Do you keep horses in your hall?" ' Mrs Powell added, 'I ask them at what time they were disturbed, and when they always reply, "Two o'clock", I know it is the phantom.'

One visitor to the hotel was so fascinated by the ghostly sound that he engaged in a considerable amount of research to try and discover what historical fact might lie behind it. According to his investigations into old records, it was found that after William and Mary of Orange came to take over the throne of England in 1689, they planned to visit Dartmouth which has always been important because of its naval tradition. The King was to come by ship but, because she suffered from seasickness, Queen Mary travelled down from London by road and stayed at the Royal Castle where she waited for her husband's ship to arrive.

William's vessel was delayed by fog and, instead of landing at Dartmouth, it had to put into nearby Brixham. As the Queen had wanted to receive the King personally, a courier was despatched as the King's ship came into port. He was followed by a coach which must have pulled up in a narrow cobbled lane that ran between the inn and another house. And for some inexplicable reason the sounds of that coach and its outrider have echoed down to the 20th century.

45

'So my husband was not far wrong,' Mrs Powell said. 'In his abnormal state he somehow tried to tie up the supernatural experience with modern times, and he was anxious in case our receptionist might not inform the Queen.'

Mrs Powell explained that later on the inn had been joined to the neighbouring building and, where the lane used to be, there is now the foyer of the hotel which explains why the coach sounds as though it goes right through the centre of the building.

Although Queen Mary's coach has never been seen, Mrs Powell said she had witnessed another ghostly manifestation at the Royal Castle.

'Sometimes, when I have closed up the drawing room at night, I have seen a rather nasty little man on the stairs,' she explained. 'He's small like a jockey, and he always gives me a malicious grin. The first time it was a bit alarming, but he has never done me any harm and I'm used to him now. I mentioned it to an old customer once, and she said, "Why, that's Darkie Chase! He was an ostler who used to live in the inn stables. Everyone thought he was a little odd because he used to claim he could commune with the spirits."

'I am not sure whether I see him in my mind or with my eyes but, either way, he appears real enough. Like the coach, he comes in spasms.'

WHO'D HAVE THOUGHT IT
(Milton Coombe. Map reference: 169)

'There are one or two people in the village who have seen the ghost,' said Frances Rowe, landlady of this curiously named pub. 'There is a half-canopy bed in one of the bedrooms and people do say that he has been seen in that room.'

The ghost in the bedroom is that of a cavalier who has been described as 'sad faced'. He is not alone. According to printed information available at the inn, 'Many tales are told of ghosts that have been spotted down the centuries including a couple of former landlords . . .'

The same notes give the explanation for the pub's name: 'Formerly called The Welcome, the inn got its present and unusual name when, in the face of competition from another establishment in the village, it was granted a spirits' licence. As the favoured landlord rushed out holding the excise licence a cry of "Who'd have thought it!" went up from the crowd outside including the rival landlord, and the scene is depicted on the inn sign.'

Dorset

THE ANGEL
(Lyme Regis. Map reference: 4)

The medieval port of Lyme Regis has witnessed many fascinating events. King Edward I used its harbour, thus giving it its royal title, when he was at war with the French, and it was here in 1685 that the Duke of Monmouth landed to lead his ill-starred insurrection against James II. Following this, the town became a haunt of smugglers and, in 1811, Mary Anning, a carpenter's daughter, made history by finding the first skeleton of an *icthyosaurus* (a marine reptile which lived up to 120 million years ago) in a cliff face near the town.

Part of Jane Austen's novel *Persuasion* was set in Lyme Regis, and the house in which she wrote it is still standing. In our own time John Fowler added to its literary immortality by making it the setting for *The French Lieutenant's Woman*.

The supernatural element crept into the town's history in the summer of 1967, when the *Bridport News* reported ghostly phenomena in the middle of the town centring around the Angel Inn. From reading the newspaper accounts I expected some sort of poltergeist activity when I visited the Angel, but the landlady, Mrs Mabs Noble, told me she believed the ghost was that of a widow who had formerly kept the Angel.

Things are mysteriously moved around the inn, an activity which many hotel ghosts seem to indulge in.

'I feel no animosity from the ghost,' Mrs Noble declared, 'and I have never been frightened. The funny thing is I have not seen her, yet I have the feeling that I am never alone. It may sound strange but being a widow myself, and with my son at boarding school, I find the presence rather comforting.'

The ghost sometimes manifests itself by opening the inner door of the bar after it has been bolted, but Mrs Noble said, 'I think she has suffered personal unhappiness and is now comforting me. I feel a protective influence from her.'

THE BARLEY MOW
(Broomhill. Map reference: 9)

It is comparatively rare for a ghost or similar psychic phenomenon to be seen by more than one person at a time. An example of a rare group sighting was reported in the press in 1979 when the landlord of the Barley Mow, David Parker, and five members of his staff were clearing up the bar after closing at Christmas time.

'Suddenly we all felt something completely different,' Mr Parker was reported as saying. 'There was a sort of shapeless haze over the fireplace. It disappeared after only thirty seconds, but everyone noticed it. We couldn't really work out what had happened. It was a strange and rather frightening sensation.'

It was the second appearance of the haze. Two years earlier Mr Parker and his wife had seen it.

A link between the phenomenon and Oliver Cromwell has been suggested. During the Civil War, when the Barley Mow was a humble drover's cottage, Cromwell's troops were billeted beside it and before going into battle they were blessed by a minister in a road nearby which is now called God's Blessing Lane. But why this should cause the appearance of a 'shapeless haze' in the 20th century is likely to remain unclear.

THE CROWN
(Poole. Map reference: 48)

'We bolted down the stairs which led to the courtyard. We had been there only a couple of minutes when this fluorescent mist – about the size of a child's head – came downstairs towards us.'

In these words Eric Drayman described a supernatural happening which took place at a public house in Poole in June 1966. He had been standing with two friends, Paul Eeles and Malcolm Squire, in the courtyard of the Crown Hotel in Market Street, when all three heard a single note being played on a piano in the upper room of an old stable – a room which was being renovated so it could be used for dancing.

'When we heard the piano, Paul, who lived at the hotel, told

49

me it was a ghost,' said Malcolm Squire. 'I thought he was pulling my leg.'

The young men went up the stairs to investigate but found the room to be deserted.

'No one was in the room yet, somehow, this one note on the piano was being struck,' continued Mr Squire. 'Suddenly, everything on top of the piano showered on the floor and the front of the piano collapsed.'

At this, they ran down the stairs, and a few moments later the 'fluorescent mist' was seen to float down the steps, then drift across the courtyard until it disappeared at the hotel entrance. An Australian guest at The Crown, Mr D. Browne, thought that what they had seen was a trick of the imagination and decided to prove it.

He carefully bolted the door, painted five crosses on it and went down into the courtyard. Two minutes later the door opened by itself.

'It was the most eerie feeling I have ever had in my life,' the Australian told the *Poole and Dorset Herald* which ran the story on the front page of its edition of 22 June.

No explanation was found for the strange episode although the landlord of the Crown Hotel, Alan Brown, believed that the activity was triggered off by the alterations being made to the stable room.

THE ROYAL LION HOTEL
(Lyme Regis. Map reference: 4)

The strange experiences of four young members of the Royal Lion's staff caused the hotel to become news in the local press in the summer of 1973. The phenomena they experienced ranged from the disembodied moaning of a woman in distress to a white shape which appeared like 'a drifting mist or stream'.

A reporter from the *Bridport and Lyme Regis News* interviewed Alan Jones and his wife Susan and another couple, Markus and Geraldine de Roseus, about the happenings which had alarmed them during the short period they had been living on the premises. Markus de Roseus described how late one night he had heard the kitchen door slam and then disembodied footsteps approached him across the darkened dining-room. As they came nearer and nearer he lost his nerve and fled.

His colleagues agreed that such paranormal activity produced a sensation of cold. Susan Jones said, 'It's like a damp mist going right through you, turning you to jelly.'

Something which both couples experienced was a sound of moaning which they heard in their bedrooms situated on opposite sides of a courtyard. It was described as continuing endlessly through the night, though at times it was replaced by the sound of an organ. Only once, however, had anything out of the ordinary been seen and this was the white shape glimpsed by Alan and Susan Jones.

'We're all frightened to death,' Mr Jones was reported as saying. 'We just can't understand it.'

The newspaper reporter suggested that an explanation for the phenomena might have a connection with the Royal Lion's past when part of it contained dungeons for prisoners who were tried at the courthouse next door. Occasionally the courtyard was used as an execution site and it could be that the moaning goes back to that time.

East Sussex

DEANS PLACE HOTEL
(Alfriston. Map reference: 54)

Alfriston, with its 14th century cross-shaped church and picture book Clergy House, is one of the show villages of Sussex. In the summer its long narrow street is thronged with visitors in search of afternoon tea and antiques. The village has two ghostly traditions. The first is a spectre wearing a grey dress. She has been described as a 'vague little creature', and has been seen to emerge from the vicarage and to vanish on approaching St Andrew's Church.

The village's other ghost is the Blue Lady of Deans Place Hotel. Unfortunately she has outlasted her story and, apart from a vague idea that she was a murder victim, no one can give an explanation for her appearances. But there is no doubt that this lady in a long old fashioned dress of blue material has been glimpsed by hotel guests.

THE KING'S ARMS
(Rotherfield. Map reference: 90)

When you enter the King's Arms you find yourself in one of England's most beautiful inn interiors. Its ancient oaken beams – black with age and hard as iron – came from a dismantled sailing ship; the ceiling rafters still retain the curve of the ship's ribs.

The history of the building began when it was constructed as the tithe house next to the manor, after which it became a bakery. According to one legend an unhappy miller ended his life here by hanging himself from one of the rafters. Logically it should be his spirit which haunts the inn, but the spectre which has been glimpsed there is that of a young woman whose story is shrouded in mystery.

In 1751 the bakery was turned into a hostelry. Here stayed Samuel Pepys who complained of the cost of his breakfast, perhaps a little unreasonably in view of the fact he had demanded special black silk sheets for his bed.

When I visited the King's Arms, the landlord Reginald Lloyd told me of his disappointment at not having seen the inn's ghost which is traditionally expected to appear every Midsummer Night's eve.

'We are supposed to be haunted by the ghost of a young lady,' he said. 'She was the daughter of a landlord here at the turn of the century, but even the oldest regulars have no idea why she should want to revisit her former home.

'Although I have not had the luck to see her myself – and I have stayed up several Midsummer Night's eves in the hope of doing so – I know an ex-landlord of this place who swears he had a strange experience.

'His name was Peterson, and being an ex-Marine Commander he was not the sort of man to give in easily to night fancies. The room he used as his office was the one in which the ghost of the young lady had been seen to appear, and when the bar closed he would go up there with his dogs to make up the books.

'One night he entered the room and found it inexplicably cold, while the dogs bristled with fear and refused to enter. He said it was more than a physical cold, it seemed to enter his very being – and it scared the life out of him!

'He came downstairs and it took several stiff brandies to pull himself together. Although people laughed when he told them of his experience, he always remained convinced that the strange drop in temperature, and the feeling of fright which accompanied it, were related to the ghost.'

THE LAMB
(Eastbourne. Map reference: 97)

For connoisseurs of fine old English inns The Lamb in Eastbourne's Old Town is a joy. In its large rooms, whose ceilings are supported by genuine Tudor beams of black oak, logs blaze in the fireplaces and thankfully there is not the electronic bleep of a Space Invader nor the beat of a juke box to disturb the murmur of conversation.

The inn sign outside has 'AD 1180' painted on it, while below ground there is an excellent example of a vaulted undercroft which merchants may have used to keep their bales of cloth safe. In the cellar next to this subterranean dome there is a deep and mysterious shaft which possibly had something to do with the secret tunnels which legend says once ran from the inn.

It would almost be impossible for such a place not to have a supernatural tradition, and The Lamb's new landlord Harold Bailey – who until recently had been landlord of the Shakespeare Hotel in Manchester which is also written up in this book – told me that there was a room with a strange reputation on the top floor.

I was shown a letter written in 1977 by a Mrs Lillian Hart who as a young girl stayed at the inn when her uncle was the publican.

'There is a room which I hated being in while dusting,' she wrote. 'My cousin was supposed to have scoffed at this and definitely felt the bed lift in the night, and wouldn't sleep there again.'

Apart from this presence in the upper storey, it is possible that The Lamb was connected with a haunting which took place in an old house across the road which was supposed to have been linked to the inn by one of its legendary passages.

Mrs Duffus, the lady who lived there before the Second World War, acquired a richly carved font, said to have been of Saxon origin, which was installed as an ornamental bowl on the ground floor. She told friends that it attracted the ghost of a portly monk. When the haunting became too much for her she contacted Bishop Bell, then Bishop of Chichester, who called and advised her to remove it. By 1945 it had gone from her home though Mrs Duffus would not say how, merely that she was happy that the monk no longer appeared.

It is possible that the monk could have been once associated with The Lamb which is thought to have had ecclesiastical beginnings as the inn sign of a haloed lamb bearing a cross suggests.

THE MERMAID
(Rye. Map reference: 104)

The Mermaid is one of Britain's most picturesque inns, situated in one of its most picturesque small towns. The hotel has such a charming old-world look that one feels there ought to be a colourful ghost to go with it – a swashbuckling retired buccaneer or a tough old smuggler would be just right, especially as in the old days of the so-called freetraders the inn was used by that bane of the excise, the Hawkhurst gang.

In fact the Mermaid was once reputed to be haunted by the ghost of a 'freetrader', who came to an untimely end, as well as the phantom of a girl who unwisely gave her heart to a member of his fraternity. I understand from the landlord that nothing paranormal has occurred lately, so perhaps like so many other phantoms these two have faded away.

But there is one other story concerning the Mermaid which appeared in a pamphlet about the inn. Apparently there was an old tradition that each night of 29 October a haunting took place in the Elizabethan Room. On one such night two ladies – one claiming to be psychic – slept in the room to see if anything unusual would happen. During the night the non-psychic lady awoke – her friend remained asleep through the episode – and saw two men dressed in doublet and hose fighting a duel with swords. The lady watched while one of the combatants ran his sword through his opponent's body. He then picked up the corpse and dropped it out of sight down a shaft in the corner of the room.

When the spectator regained her composure she looked in the corner and found that the hole in the floor had been long sealed up.

THE REGENCY TAVERN
(Brighton. Map reference: 132)

Landlady Jackie Penfold is disappointed not to have encountered the ghosts which long haunted this tavern standing in Regency Square. A reason for her disappointment might be that the ghosts gave up haunting following an occasion some time ago, reported in the *Brighton Argus* which said, 'It took a special session by a medium with spiritually attuned friends to lay to rest the psychic manifestations.'

'Actually there were two ghosts,' said Jackie Penfold. 'One was a landlady from bygone days who has been seen in the cellar. And one of the upstairs rooms has been haunted by a sixteen-year-old girl with long black hair who threw herself out of the window.'

THE RINGMER INN
(Ringmer. Map reference: 136)

Sid is the nickname of the poltergeist which was written up in the *Publican* at the end of 1979 after it became a nuisance at the Ringmer Inn. Sid caused bottles to jump off bar shelves, also he was blamed for turning off the gas in the cellar and for making stomping sounds on the landing.

'I think it is friendly, but I want to get rid of it because it is becoming a damn nuisance,' said landlord Roger Lavendon. 'For a start we have to keep going down into the cellar to turn the gas back on. We have been doing a lot of alterations and I think the banging must have disturbed it.'

When members of the Sussex Ghost Hunters Club spent a night at the Ringmer Inn Sid tired of his tricks and from then on peace returned to the pub.

Essex

THE ANGEL
(Braintree. Map reference: 2)

Some of the most intriguing supernatural activity to take place in a pub has occurred at The Angel, one of the oldest buildings in Braintree, where the house entity takes a critical interest in the decor of the premises. The haunting became news some years ago when a new landlord took over and began altering the pub and re-decorating it. One of his innovations was the erection of a new sign. It depicted a woman, 'more like a witch than an angel, with wings and a halo', quaffing a merry pint while riding a bomb rather as a witch rode a broomstick – the bomb commemorated the fact that the pub had had a near-miss during an air raid.

This flamboyant portrait of an angel created consternation in the town. A heavenly being with a beer glass in her hand seemed sacrilegious to many, and letters to the local newspaper strongly reflected this view – a view which was shared by a ghost who soon made its displeasure felt. The story spread that the manifestations were caused by the spirit of a former landlord whose dying request was that his beloved Angel should remain as it was.

Ian Groves, son of the present landlord, told me how the ghost expressed his disapproval.

'The haunting only happens when the place is being altered,' he said. 'The ghost certainly did not like the new sign and all sorts of odd things began to happen. One example was about seven years ago when the then-landlord started to build an extension on to the back. One day there were great piles of plasterboard leaning against the bar when all of a sudden – although there was no living person near it – it was pushed over. Such disturbances always happened while the builders were actually at work. In the end they had to do the building late at night – the disturbances were such that a lot of people wouldn't come here.'

As frequently happens in haunted pubs there was a surge of supernatural activity when a new landlord took over.

'When we came two years ago I found the things that happened quite scaring at first,' said Ian Groves. 'My mother saw something come down the stairs one night which was not a living person, and once I saw an ashtray fly off the bar by itself. Other things moved around and I heard invisible people walking and talking.

'I used to sleep in a small room which had been locked up when we came to view the pub. When I was there I heard people walking up and down. This used to keep me awake so I moved into the next room. But I liked the small room and wanted to go back, so I decided to decorate it in its original style and colours. I took up the lino and polished the old floorboards and put old furniture in there. It seems to me that the ghost likes the place as it used to be because since then nothing has happened in there.'

Another indication of approval was shown by a change in temperature. When the Groves took over The Angel they found that despite central heating in the small room, it was 'always freezing cold' but since the return to its earlier state it has been warm.

'In the corner of the saloon bar – beneath my haunted bedroom – I have always sensed there is some invisible presence,' said Ian Groves. 'There is a tradition that it is a ghostly nun from a convent which was supposed to stand here, but I have an odd feeling that it is a couple of children.

'To me the strangest aspect of it all was the premonitions I used to get in that room. I found I just knew that certain things were going to happen and I told people about them, and I've got witnesses to prove that I had been right.'

On one occasion he dreamed of somebody being involved in a car accident, and next day it happened.

'I had dreamed that it had happened to me, and that I was in a hospital room with doctors standing round the bed looking at me,' he said. 'After it actually happened I went to see the injured driver in a hospital I had never visited before. There I recognised the room and the doctors though, of course, it was no longer me on the bed.

'Ghost hunting parties come to The Angel from time to time, but things are quiet now. It seems as though whatever it is approves of how we have restored the place. We have a proper angel on the sign now.'

THE BEAR INN
(Stock. Map reference: 11)

One of the most famous of England's haunted pubs is the Bear Inn, perhaps because it is a favourite of the author James Wentworth Day who has written about it – and its ghost – so affectionately.

'Where's Spider?' visitors to the inn who know the story invariably ask. 'Is he still up the chimney?'

At the end of last century Spider Marshall was The Bear's diminutive ostler, and his nickname – inspired by his curious scuttling gait – was regarded as particularly apt when he performed his extraordinary party piece which earned him countless pints. This consisted of Spider entering the fireplace in the tap room and squeezing his small body up the chimney.

It is believed that there is a small chamber, known as a bacon loft, in this four-centuries-old building into which the flues from the tap room and the bar parlour both enter. Certainly the two chimneys were joined because Spider, having vanished in the tap room, would suddenly appear like a soot-grimed imp in the fireplace of the parlour to the applause and cheers of the customers.

Sometimes Spider became temperamental as a performer, especially when plenty of pints had come his way, and having climbed the chimney he would remain up there in the hot darkness, ignoring the shouts which floated up from below. Often the regulars forced him to return by lighting straw in the fireplace, roaring with laughter when a furious Spider appeared cursing out of the smoke. But one Christmas Eve things got out of hand. Spider as usual was lost to sight up the chimney, and once he had reached his perch he refused to return. Perhaps he had been treated to so many seasonal drinks he fell asleep. Whatever the reason, he made no response when the usual straw was ignited below him.

When this failed more drastic action was taken. Faggots were piled in the fireplace and set ablaze, but Spider never came down . . .

It is believed that he was suffocated by the smoke and that his smoke-cured body is still up there in some black chimney recess. But if Spider's mortal remains are safely out of sight, his phantom has been seen at the Bear Inn, recognised by his scuttling walk, jockey-like body and white breeches. And he is still a popular character at the inn. Each Christmas a special ceremonial toast is drunk in his memory.

THE BELL HOTEL
(Thorpe-le-Soken. Map reference: 14)

This hotel has been the scene of the sort of poltergeist activity which is quite common in many haunted British pubs. On the other hand it can boast a phantom unique in that she was a bigamist who died in the 18th century and was buried in a churchyard close by.

THE CROSS KEYS HOTEL
(Saffron Walden. Map reference: 45)

Charles Dickens would have loved the Cross Keys. In appearance it is a splendid example of a timbered building such as one would see in illustrations out of the *Pickwick Papers*. It has a nice touch of eccentricity in that when it was constructed five centuries ago it was done so round a tree, and historically it can hold its own as a favourite rendezvous for Parliamentarian officers when Cromwell made his headquarters at Saffron Walden. But above all, it has a Christmas ghost.

In the past landlords have reported that the haunting occurs between 11 pm and midnight on Christmas Eve. This takes the form of heavy footsteps made by some invisible entity in the upper floor of the hotel. Each time they are heard the description is identical, and what is curious is that they move along a passage which ends with a blank wall.

THE GOLDEN FLEECE
(Brentwood. Map reference: 75)

A woman guest once staying at the Golden Fleece had an alarming experience when she happened to look into her bedroom mirror. In the glass she saw the cowled figure of a monk standing behind her. She spun round to confront the intruder, only to find that the room was empty. That in itself was bad enough, but worse was to follow. Turning back to the mirror she saw that the sinister figure was still reflected there!

The fact that a spectral monk has been seen there from time to time is in keeping with the history of the pub as it was built on the site of a 12th century priory.

THE KING'S HEAD
(Ongar. Map reference: 92)

Proud of being the oldest pub in the town, the King's Head was once the scene of a puzzling manifestation. A previous publican and his wife were awakened one night by a greenish radiance shining beneath their door. Thinking that the corridor outside must be lit up, the landlord went to investigate, but on opening the door he found the deserted passage to be in utter darkness. The following morning an excited guest told him about a strange green glow she had seen beneath her door . . .

No explanation for the eerie light was ever found.

SAINT ANNE'S CASTLE INN
(Great Leighs. Map reference: 142)

In White's *Gazetteer of Essex* it is stated that the inn was formerly a hermitage known as Saint Anne's where pilgrims from Walsingham, on their way to the shrine of Saint Thomas à Becket, took their rest. Today the inn sign shows a skull wearing a mitre representing Thomas à Becket together with the date of his birth, and a scene of pilgrims coming over a hill.

The haunting of the inn began with an incident worthy of the opening scene in a Hammer horror film. The stone above a

61

witch's grave was removed, thus releasing a malignantly mischievous force which had been trapped there since the days when Essex earned its reputation as the Witch County. According to the inn's proprietor, Dennis Higginson, this is the entity which haunts the inn.

'It is a fact that a witch was executed in this village long ago,' he explained. 'She was buried with a stake through her heart at Scrap Faggot Green and a boulder was placed over her grave, no doubt with the idea that it would keep her safely buried.'

Later I found Scrap Faggot Green to be a small triangle of turf where three roads join in a Y junction down a side road which runs from the main road past the Saint Anne's Castle Inn. This would be in keeping with the witch legend as a burial place, such people being interred in unhallowed ground and, preferably, at a crossroads.

'The story about the witch being killed here is quite authentic,' Mr Higginson continued. 'The name bears it out, too. "Scrap Faggot" is the old Essex name for a witch.

'During the last war there were a lot of big American military trucks in this area. They were too long and too large to get round Scrap Faggot Green. They bulldozed away the boulder in the middle of it so they could drive straight across the grass. From then on peculiar things began to happen in the village, often quite comical things. I'll give you one example: One farmer had quite a few hens and another chap up the road had a lot of ducks. When they got up one morning the chap who owned the hens found he had the ducks while the duck owner had the hens. You might say it was an ordinary practical joker, but have you ever tried to catch dozens of ducks at night without making any noise?'

Whether this was a supernatural joke or not, such tampering with livestock is the sort of thing that witches used to be accused of in Essex.

'The spirit of the witch was released by the removal of the stone, and we think that it took up residence in this pub,' said Mr Higginson. 'Strange things have happened here, some of them quite frightening. I remember on one occasion, a drayman came from the Romford brewery which supplies our stuff. I left him alone in the cellar putting the beer out. When I returned he had jumped out of the cellar and stood shaking by his dray.

"I'm never going into your cellar again," he said. "Don't be stupid, Jock," I said. "Come on, now." "Not likely," he answered. "Not after that thing standing behind me." And, since then, Jock refuses to come on this round.'

There have been other similar incidents at Saint Anne's but the most dramatic related to a young girl.

'It was one Sunday lunchtime,' the proprietor said. 'A local farmer from down the road – one of my regulars – had come in with his daughter and her girl friend who had not been in the pub before. She was about seventeen. While the farmer had a drink down here, the girls spent the time playing darts in the top bar. It got to closing time and the pub cleared except for old Bill, the farmer, and a couple of others.

'The girls came down through the doorway from the top bar so that they could get a lift home with the father. The daughter's friend looked in the fireplace (it was summer and it had been cleared out) and gave a dreadful scream.

'Carole – that's old Bill's daughter – said, "What on earth's the matter?" And the girl said: "Look at that thing in the fireplace!" And then she fell to the floor in a faint. There was nothing there that we could see, but she saw something which was enough to scare her into unconsciousness. She could never say clearly what it was, just a shape like a human figure standing in the large fireplace beneath the chimney. Since that day she has never set foot in this place again.'

THE SWAN
(Brentwood. Map reference: 75)

At Wilson's Corner in Brentwood a tall obelisk marks the spot where William Hunter was burnt to death for his religious faith during the reign of Bloody Mary. Inscribed on its base are these words: *He being dead yet speaketh*. They are strangely appropriate because, although the ghost of the martyr does not actually make sounds, his actions speak for themselves when he haunts The Swan which stands in the High Street.

I had not been in the bar long before an old regular was telling me about the strange happenings there.

'It's Mr Hunter, as we call him,' he said. 'He makes things

happen. Do you see those big copper plates on that shelf up there? I've seen them roll along all by themselves. It was as though someone was pushing them, but there was no one there that we could see.'

Daphne Thorp, wife of landlord John Thorp, explained that William Hunter had been imprisoned at The Swan before his execution. According to an account left by his brother, the young man (he was nineteen at the time) had a vivid dream the night before he was taken to the stake. In it he foresaw the events of the following morning, how he met his father who blessed him and how, when he went to the place where the faggots were being piled round the stake, the sheriff showed him a letter from the Queen saying that, if he recanted, he would be spared. In his dream the youth refused and was chained to the heavy post.

As the chain was tightened, he cried out: 'Son of God, shine upon me!' At these words, the sun suddenly appeared from behind a cloud and a sunbeam illuminated the figure of the martyr, much to the awe of the silent onlookers.

Next day, 26 March 1555, everything happened as William had dreamed it. Just before the torch was applied to the brushwood and faggots, a priest came forward with a 'popish book' to give the prisoner a final chance to renounce his faith, but he cried, 'Away, false prophet!' The next minute he was hidden from view by the smoke and flame.

Since then his restless spirit has frequently revisited the scene of his last imprisonment.

'No one has ever seen him but we have heard bumping sounds, quite unaccountable, coming from the cellar,' Mrs Thorp said. 'Sometimes furniture is moved about mysteriously during the night, and the lights are switched on and off. Many people have noticed something peculiar about the stairs which lead up from the cellar to the top of the building. There are sudden drops in the temperature and the feeling of a cold "presence".'

She added that she was not frightened of the ghost. 'I have every sympathy for him,' she said. 'It has been suggested that we have him exorcised, but I would not dream of it.'

The most haunted part of The Swan, which used to be a coaching inn in days gone by, is an upstairs bedroom where it is believed William Hunter spent his last night and dreamed of his forthcoming execution. When the Thorps moved into the inn, their daughter, Carla, was given this room, but its supernatural activity upset her so much that she was unable to face spending any more nights at The Swan.

Gloucestershire

THE BLACK HORSE
(Cirencester. Map reference: 22)

The dramatic haunting of the Black Horse Inn, believed to be the oldest public house in Cirencester, can be traced in the files of the *Vale of White Horse Gazette* for 1933. It broke the story in its edition of 18 August under the headlines: HOTEL BEDROOM GHOST – CIRENCESTER WOMAN ALARMED BY PHANTOM VISITOR – THE WRITING ON THE WINDOW.

The newspaper report told how on the night of Sunday the 13th Miss Ruby Bower, whose uncle and aunt held the licence of the Black Horse, awoke at midnight with a strange feeling. She felt fearful and uneasy before she opened her eyes. This changed to a sensation of terror when she did so because the room was bathed in an unearthly light.

A rustling sound in a corner of the room caused her to look up and, according to the paper:

> . . . her horror increased as she beheld an apparition in the shape of a stout old lady with an evil face and a grim expression, gliding slowly across the floor. Despite her fears, and the fact that the whole thing could not have lasted more than a fraction of a second, every detail of the scene is indelibly impressed on Miss Bower's memory. She recalls the old-fashioned clothes of the midnight visitor, the long fawn-coloured dress of a stiff silk that rustled as the old lady moved, the white apron with its frills, and the white frilly mob cap. In her hands was something which Miss Bower was unable to distinguish.
>
> Miss Bower, who was now sitting up in bed, screamed out: 'No! No! Don't, don't!'

At the sound of this cry the ghost vanished, apparently walking through the opposite wall of the room. As the phantom disappeared so the strange radiance which filled the room was extinguished and Miss Bower was left in darkness. The account added that the strange part of Miss Bower's story was that her room had recently undergone considerable alterations. A long panel had been built, forming a passage between the room and an outside wall in which there was a window, yet when Miss Bower awoke the panel seemed to have gone and her room appeared as it was before the alteration so she was able to see the window on the outside wall. Apparently she was so sure she had seen this window that, when her panic was past, she put out her hand and, on finding the panelling still there, was very surprised.

When she told her uncle and aunt the story they immediately went to her bedroom where a second, and perhaps even more mysterious, aspect of the story became apparent.

The bedroom was searched and nothing unusual was noticed until they came to the window which was made up of a number of small panes. One of the panes had been scratched with a diamond in the form of old-fashioned handwriting. The name 'John' appeared to have been written several times by this means.

The *Vale of White Horse Gazette* commented:

> Disbelievers would say that the writing on the window was there before Sunday – the night of the ghost's visitation – but the landlord of the hotel is confident that it was not there previously. Since he and his wife had frequently cleaned the window in question, it is inconceivable that they would not have noticed it.
>
> Apparently the scratches formed part of an attempt to cut a signature into the glass and, curiously enough, the scratching is obviously new – not having assumed the dark appearance common to cuts that have been made in glass for some time.

No explanation could be given for the sudden appearance of this writing on the window pane. Regarding the ghost, Mr and Mrs Bower put forward a theory that, during recent renovations to the hotel, a treasure which was traditionally buried there was nearly found. The old lady had to find a new hiding place. Mr Bower told a newspaper reporter that his niece was not a fanciful girl and, apart from the treasure theory, there was no reason why the ghost should appear in her room.

The newspaper took up the story again in its issue of 25 August under the heading: WILL THE GHOST WALK AGAIN? – SPECIAL INVESTIGATION OF CIRENCESTER MYSTERY – COWLED FIGURES AND AN OLD CHAPEL.

The story beneath this heading said that, although no final explanation of the phantom visitor had been reached, considerable light had been thrown on the mysterious phenomena by the services of a lady – referred to as Mrs X – who was reputed to be invested with psychic powers. According to the newspaper she made some astonishing revelations, a number of which were subsequently proved correct.

The *Gazette* reporter wrote:

> I met Mrs X at a house in Cricklade Street, Cirencester. She wishes to remain nameless but has authorised me to state that she lives within ten miles of the town, and that she is well known to be possessed of certain psychic powers.
>
> After a short argument, which concluded with Mrs X giving permission to a member of the *Gazette* to be present at her investigations, the procession – which included two lady residents of Cirencester – started for the Black Horse Inn.
>
> Mrs X had no idea where the inn was situated, and one of the ladies headed the party.

As the small group turned from Cricklade Street into Castle Street where the Black Horse stands, Mrs X apparently stopped dead and grasped the reporter by the arm. 'We are not alone,' she said, 'there are people moving all around us – people in cowls, some in brown and some in white.'

When the small procession arrived at the inn Mrs X said to Mrs Bower, 'This has all been changed. The entrance used to be through the room on the right.'

'Quite right,' replied Mrs Bower. 'It was altered many years ago.'

From then on the mysterious Mrs X proceeded to provide the reporter with all the copy he could wish for. An inspection was made of the ground floor which went quite normally until the party came to a room at the back. Here Mrs X was seen to stagger and cling to the doorway.

'I can't go in there,' she cried. Then as she went up the stairs to the first floor she said: 'This has been altered just here,' and Mrs Bower agreed that this was so. At the door of room Number 3 on the first floor Mrs X again showed signs of distress and said she was unable to enter. In the next room a dramatic change came over her.

The reporter wrote:

> She seemed to wither, her back bowed and her left leg was twisted inwards. The fingers of her right hand twisted and grasped some strange object. Her voice was that of an old woman. Her words came slowly. 'I feel sad,' she murmured, 'very, very sad. I have a terrible pain in my leg. I cannot walk properly. I have a stick in my hand. I tap on the floor with it.'
>
> Still limping Mrs X went from room to room until she finally straightened her back and became almost 'her normal self' although throughout the rest of the proceedings she was unable to straighten her leg and the foot was twisted into a grotesque position.

The party then went up the stairs to the second floor to the room where Ruby Bower had had her ghostly experience.

At the top of the stairs Mrs X said: 'I see a crucifix in front of me just there,' and she pointed half left and to the front of her. At the small door leading into an attic she said again that she was unable to enter.

As she approached the haunted room Mrs X repeated that there was a crucifix nearby. When the party opened the door there upon a chest of drawers beside the bed were three crucifixes.

'There is no harm meant in this room,' said Mrs X to Miss Bower. 'You have nothing to fear in here. I cannot quite get the story clear but there was an old man and an old lady. The old lady has a long chin and long beak-like nose. She is earthbound, she has done the old man some injury and wanders about the house. But the harm she would do or has done is not in this room. It is in one of the rooms I could not enter.'

The story of the Black Horse haunting was kept alive in the next week's edition of the *Gazette* by a photograph of the hotel. In reference to the scratchings on the glass pane the caption under the photograph said: 'Is it possible that these hieroglyphics may be explained in the light of an extract from St Clair Baddeleys' *History of Cirencester*? This states "Castell Strete, where lived the Arnolds, Porters, Mores and Cokes". The name scratched on the windowpane may well be John Coke. Can this lady have been some spirit descendant of the Cokes who probably lived in this house years ago?'

The activities of this medium, our old friend Mrs X, were reported in the issue of 8 September under the headline CIRENCESTER GHOST LAID. According to the report, a lady correspondent of the newspaper had received a message from Mrs X telling her she had become aware that the ghost could be 'laid' if certain measures were strictly followed. At exactly 3 pm on the third day of the month three white flowers must be laid in Number 3 bedroom – not the room in which the ghost was seen but that one which Mrs X was unable to enter on the first floor of the inn.

'At about ten minutes to three on September the third,' the lady correspondent wrote, 'Mrs X, myself, the landlord of the Black Horse and his wife, assembled in the bar parlour of the inn. We waited in silence for a few moments and then Mrs X suddenly said: "The circle is not yet complete." A little later she again spoke, remarking this time: "It's now complete. An old lady has joined us." '

Mrs X then led the way up the stairs carrying three white gladioli. This time she was able to enter Number 3 bedroom and almost at once she said: 'I see two windows in front of me.'

This was thought to be an extraordinary statement as Mrs X was facing a wall but it was later ascertained that had she stood on the spot years ago before some alterations were made she would have been able to see two windows in front of her. She laid down the three white flowers in the room and then said that providing the room was not entered or opened for three whole days the ghost would be finally laid and would worry the occupants of the inn no longer.

When I visited the Black Horse I stayed in the room where Ruby Bowers had seen her apparition. It was close to

Christmas time and Cirencester, often styled the capital of the Cotswolds, appeared like an illustration for a Charles Dickens' Christmas story. The rambling inn turned out to be a delightful place which has been in use since 1470. Before that the building had belonged to a wool merchant who used it for stapling and storing his wool.

I asked the landlord, John Griffiths, if the treasure mentioned in the *Vale of White Horse Gazette* had ever been discovered.

'I'm afraid not,' he replied, 'although when that area was dug up, a lot of Roman remains were found which are now in the Cirencester museum.'

Next I asked him if the efforts of the publicity-shy Mrs X had been successful in ending the haunting of the hotel.

'Not really,' he said. 'About twelve years ago a lady here saw a ghost. She was in the bar and looking across saw a lady in grey. She said she thought she was waiting to be served but the apparition suddenly vanished.'

On another occasion a London hospital sister was staying in the haunted room. Her fiancé was sleeping in the next door room when he suddenly heard her cry out. He dashed to the next room and found she was in a state of terror having seen an apparition. He spent the rest of the night on guard, sitting in the corridor with his back against the door of the haunted room but nothing further happened.

The mysterious pane of glass on which the word 'John' is scratched is still to be seen in the haunted bedroom, as enigmatic today as it was when it made newspaper headlines.

YE OLD CORNER CUPBOARD
(Winchcombe. Map reference: 109)

This quaintly named pub goes back nine centuries to when it was part of the local abbey, yet for once such an establishment is not haunted by a monk from pre-Dissolution days. The haunting here is the sound of a child's running footsteps. They come from the floor above the bar, and appear to travel the length of the building which means that they pass through a wall. Unfortunately there is no clue to the identity of the little visitor, but the reaction of those who have heard her – opinion seems to favour a little girl – is that her presence is delightful.

Greater Manchester

THE CROWN INN
(Bredbury. Map reference: 51)

The Crown Inn made news on 30 August, 1979, when the *Stockport Express* reported that it was haunted by an ill-mannered ghost – a ghost who actually *shoved* the pub's customers.

A typical example of its unpleasant behaviour was described by landlord Ken Wyatt who said, 'A chap was standing at the bar one night when he suddenly rolled round. I asked him what was the matter. "Someone's just shoved me," he replied, but there was hardly anyone in the pub at the time.'

The jostling always happened at exactly the same place in the bar. This area was the stables when the Crown was a coaching inn, and it is a local legend that a man committed suicide here by hanging himself. It is this bygone tragedy which the pub's regulars think was responsible for the unusual phenomenon.

THE JACKSON'S BOAT INN
(Chorlton-Cum-Hardy. Map reference: 85)

One of the most impressive British pub ghosts haunts this inn – he appears wearing full Highland dress.

'We call him George,' said licensee Tom Gray. 'Two of my barmaids say they have actually seen him. He has also made his presence felt in the bar by pushing glasses and bottles off the shelves.'

Perhaps the biggest mystery concerning George is why he is so far south of the Border but Mr Gray believes that it could be because the premises used to be a meeting place for Jacobites. The inn was short-listed in the recent Teacher's contest to find the most interesting and authentic haunted pubs.

THE OLDE ROCK HOUSE
(Barton-upon-Irwell. Map reference: 118)

Some years ago when floorboards were lifted in the attic of the Olde Rock House some antiquated farm labourer's clothing and an old fashioned flail were found. The proprietor was so excited by the discovery that he had the finds placed on view in a glass case.

The reason for this interest was that the objects fitted in with the legend behind the pub's curious, hard-working ghost. When seen in the past it was described as a man wearing a smock – the kind that in this modern world one associates with country yokels of bygone times – who was vigorously wielding a flail as though threshing corn. While his arm rose and fell the apparition was heard to mutter, 'Now thus, now thus!'

It was these words which gave a clue to his identity because they formed the motto of the de Trafford family. According to a local legend one of the members of this royalist clan was pursued by a detachment of Roundheads during the Civil War, and just when it seemed he could go no farther, he reached a barn close to the inn.

Inside a number of labourers were at work on the grain floor and de Trafford donned a smock and joined them. As he flailed he expressed his defiance by muttering his family motto, which fitted in quite well with the work. No doubt when the Ironsides reached the barn the foreman said the equivalent of 'He went that-a way!'

YE OLDE NO 3
(Bollington. Map reference: 119)

The name of this pub – which comes from the days when it was the third stopping place on the coach route from Liverpool – is apt because three different paranormal manifestations have been reported on its premises.

One is definitely caused by a poltergeist. An article about Ye Olde No 3 which appeared in the house magazine of a brewery described an 'ice-cold breeze' which seems to suddenly sweep through the rooms despite the fact that the windows are securely fastened and there is nowhere from which a normal draught could blow. Other phenomena described were the mysterious moving of carpets and scattering of clothing during the night, electric lights which appeared to be switched on and off by invisible fingers, and occurrences which remind one of the kind fairies in nursery tales – the cleaning and polishing of the pub's brassware after the bar had been closed for the night.

The pub's more usual haunting concerns the spectre of a gipsy girl who was drowned in a nearby stream into which she fell while fleeing from the law.

The third manifestation was seen by a landlord's wife in the early hours one morning. Something made her wake up and, looking round her bedroom, she was suddenly aware that there was an intruder – a little girl in a poke bonnet who was regarding herself intently in the mirror on the dressing-table.

'I saw her as clear as crystal,' the landlady said. 'She wore a blue frock . . .' She only realised the true nature of the small visitor when she disappeared through the door without opening it.

THE SHAKESPEARE HOTEL
(Manchester. Map reference: 146)

This hotel in Fountain Street is aptly-named for a lot of the clientele is made up of theatrical people, both locally based and visiting artists. The haunting of the premises goes back a century to when a servant girl died there tragically.

The hotel restaurant is situated on the first floor and connected to the kitchen above by a steep flight of stairs. It was the girl's job to light the kitchen ranges very early in the morning and one day, perhaps because she was still half asleep, she was careless and as a result her clothing caught fire. She panicked and ran to the top of the stairs where, surrounded by flames, she lost her footing and plunged to her death.

Since then some members of the kitchen staff, and some guests, have glimpsed her terrified phantom.

Harold Bailey, who was the landlord of The Shakespeare until the end of 1982, said, 'I had a porter leave after experiencing something odd in the kitchen. We had installed a dumb waiter beside the steep staircase to supply the restaurant below. On two different occasions when the porter went to the dumb waiter he heard sounds on the stairs, only to turn round and find that there was no one there. The second time he left my employment the same day.

'An odd thing about The Shakespeare was that no animal would stay in the building. The day we arrived our cat – who we'd had for three years – ran away and later took up residence on the other side of the street. A dog belonging to the previous publican had behaved exactly the same way on the day he had arrived, and I was told by the staff that no one had been able to bring an animal into the place.'

The strangest aspect of the hotel is the cold zones which suddenly manifest in the bar.

'One example occurred in mid-July, a beautiful day with all the windows open because the place was so warm,' said Mr Bailey. 'Something seemed to happen to a customer I had never seen before who was standing at the bar. One of my regulars saw by the expression on his face what had occurred as this was quite common at The Shakespeare. He told the stranger to take a pace to the left or to the right. The man did so and came out of the cold which was enveloping him. He stretched out his hand to where he had been standing and felt the cold again. The result was he left hurriedly, forgetting his drink.

'This has happened many, many times in different parts of the bar. A number of different psychical investigation societies have stayed overnight with all sorts of electronic equipment but they couldn't find an explanation.'

Hampshire

THE ANGEL
(Lymington. Map reference: 5)

There is one room in this ancient coaching inn which receptionist Daphne Jenkins will not enter.

'It is room No 4, one of the funniest rooms in the hotel because the floors are so uneven,' she told me. 'It is situated immediately over the archway through which the coaches used to come. Although I haven't seen the ghost myself, I don't have the courage to go into the room. When I have to take people to it, I just open the door and let them go in.'

The ghost connected with Room No 4 is that of a shadowy coachman. The Angel's other ghost has been described as 'a tall grey-haired figure wearing a naval-style uniform', to quote from the hotel's own literature. This apparition most likely goes back to the days when the inn, then known as The George, was a local for Lymington's ship-builders and the men who served in the vessels they built. There has been plenty of time for psychic phenomena to accumulate because the first inn to stand on The Angel's site was built in 1250. Today its old world charm is such that it appears in an American film to promote travel in Britain.

A curious happening was reported at The Angel during the mid-sixties. The sister-in-law of the then manager told him how surprised she was that he allowed someone to thump a piano at midnight. Because it was not proper playing there could be no question that what she had complained of was a recital coming from a guest's portable radio. What she did not know, as it was her first night in The Angel, was that the hotel's only piano had become so decrepit it had been broken up the previous day.

77

THE BRUSHMAKERS' ARMS
(Upham. Map reference: 30)

There is some doubt as to the identity of the phantom who returns to this old pub which was once used by Oliver Cromwell as his headquarters. One tradition states that it was a landlord who was brutally beaten to death for the day's takings, another that the victim was a brushmaker named Chickett. Today opinion tends to favour the brushmaker, perhaps because his story fits in well with the pub's past associations.

The Brushmakers' Arms gets its name from the fact that long before the Civil War it was the favourite meeting place for the local brushmakers who, when they had built up stocks of their witches-style brooms, would make peddling journeys to Winchester and other Hampshire towns. It is a pleasant thought to imagine these folk, in the days when the country was known as Merry England, sitting outside the inn, their fingers busy with their staves and bundles of twigs and with tankards near at hand, while those who had wearied of plaiting and binding took turns to play in the inn's skittle alley which is still in existence.

At one time the unofficial chief of the brushmakers was an old man known as Chickett. He had spent his whole life at the craft and because of his nimbleness coupled with a large round of customers, it was considered that over the years he had been able to save a small fortune. Certainly he was prosperous enough to be able to stay at the Brushmakers' Arms as a permanent guest, sleeping in a tiny room at the front of the building.

In those days banks did not exist, and every man with savings had to guard them as best he could. It was rumoured that Chickett had a small fortune in gold coins which he carried concealed on him when working or making his rounds, and which he hid under his pallet at night. No one knows how true this was but it was enough to bring some ruffians stealing into his room late one night when everyone in the inn was soundly asleep. The next morning his murdered body was found in his room, and if he had had money there was none left beneath the blood-soaked pallet. The intruders were never brought to justice, and this may have been the reason for the restless ghost's return to the scene of his killing.

Today it is said that psychic people are aware of a 'presence' when they enter the little room where the long-ago crime was committed, and dogs – those efficient barometers of the paranormal – become highly nervous if they are taken to the haunted site. The present landlord, Mike Wickham, says, 'The room still exists above the bar, and we have heard footsteps and other strange noises coming from there.'

THE CROWN HOTEL
(Alton. Map reference: 50)

The Crown Hotel is unusual in that it is one of the very few British pubs to be haunted by an animal. The story goes that a customer once got fighting drunk in the bar, and when the landlord's dog growled at him, which he must have felt was his duty as protector of the household, the man killed him. The faithful animal's body was disposed of in an old fireplace, and since then his phantom has been glimpsed about the premises.

Dogs visiting The Crown react strongly when they come near the fireplace, and a previous landlord described to a newspaper reporter how his two dogs would 'start howling and scratching at the fireplace' whenever they entered the room.

THE ECLIPSE
(Winchester. Map reference: 60)

One of the finest old buildings in Winchester is an inn called The Eclipse which was once a rectory belonging to the nearby church of Saint Laurence. It stands in the corner of the city's square close to the great cathedral, and its unusual name came about when it first became an inn. A rival establishment, the Sun Inn, was already in business opposite, and it was the new innkeeper's ambition to steal its trade. He achieved this, eclipsing The Sun, and his inn has been The Eclipse ever since.

The haunted room is right at the top of The Eclipse, its ceiling sloping with the shape of the roof while a small leaded window looks out onto the square. It was in this room that Lady Alicia

Lisle spent her last days in captivity, and here she heard the carpenters erecting the execution scaffold against the wall.

According to the *Dictionary of National Biography* Lady Alicia Lisle was the victim of a 'judicial murder'. She was at her home at Moyles Court when the Monmouth Rebellion broke out in 1685, and on 20 July she received a letter from John Hickes, a dissenting minister, asking for shelter. He did not mention he was on the run after having taken part in the Battle of Sedgemoor on 6 July.

She replied to his letter, agreeing to his request, and several days later he arrived at Moyles Court with two friends whom she did not know – nor did she know they were also wanted rebels. A prying villager saw the trio arrive and quickly informed Colonel Penruddocke who rode up with his troops the next day and arrested Lady Alicia and her guests.

On 27 August she was tried at Winchester by Judge Jeffreys on the capital charge of harbouring a traitor. In the court no evidence relating to Hickes' offences was admitted and, despite the browbeating by the judge of Dunne (one of Hickes' companions), no proof could be produced that Lady Alicia had any reason to suspect the minister of disloyalty, or that she herself had shown any sympathy towards Monmouth's insurrection.

This, plus a moderate speech by Lady Alicia on her own behalf, made the jury unwilling to convict her. But they could not stand up to the terrible judge who over-ruled their scruples, and on the following morning ordered the prisoner to be burnt at the stake that same afternoon.

The public was aghast at the sentence, and when a mob began assembling outside the judge's lodgings and the Bishop of Winchester asked for a brief reprieve, Jeffreys gave in and agreed to postpone the sentence for four days. Lady Alicia petitioned James II to change the sentence from burning. He did so, and on 22 September the old lady was publicly decapitated after she had handed the sheriff a paper denying her guilt.

She had been held at The Eclipse, and when her time came she was escorted out of a window on to the scaffold. Bravely she walked across the planks and laid her head on the block. Later, her frail body was accompanied by hundreds of

Hampshire men to Ellingham, where it was laid to rest in the local church. The procession was more of a march of triumph than a funeral cortège.

It seems that the spirit of Lady Alicia returns from time to time to visit the scene of her last few terrifying days on earth. The landlady, whose name really is Nelly Dean, told me that, although she has never experienced anything supernatural herself, she knew many people who had done so in The Eclipse.

'It is probably because I am not a psychic person,' she said, 'but there is no doubt about it, in the six years I have been here with my husband quite a few people have glimpsed the figure of a lady in grey.

'Usually when I have to put anyone into the haunted room, I don't tell them about the legend in case they are nervous. On one occasion a doctor's wife was sleeping there and in the morning she said to me over the breakfast table, "Did you hear me call out in the night?" I said, "No, what was the matter?" And she told me she had seen a grey figure of an old lady at the foot of her bed. "I was terrified," said the guest. "I called out in the hope someone would come. Then I said, 'Go away! Go away!' and at these words the figure slowly melted."

'One morning,' Mrs Dean continued, 'Edna, a girl who works here, came up to me and said, "Did you want me?" I said, "No." She said, "Well, when I was in the bathroom there was someone at the door, I thought it was you!" I replied that it wasn't me and, furthermore, there was no one else staying at the inn.

'There was also a young man who experienced something strange in the night. He was certainly a matter-of-fact, down-to-earth character, a mountaineering instructor with the Outward Bound Movement. When he came down to breakfast, he asked, "Is that room I had haunted?" I asked him why, and he replied, "Well, I had the strange feeling there was someone in the room all night. The other thing was that the temperature dropped and it was very, very cold." '

On another occasion a cleaner was vacuuming the passage with her Electrolux when she felt as though someone had put a hand on her shoulder. She turned and caught sight of something grey in the passage before it vanished.

The most dramatic appearance of Lady Alicia occurred

several years ago when a naval officer was spending a night in the haunted room. Suddenly he woke up to see the pale shadowy figure of the ghost. It upset him so much he threw his belongings into a suitcase and left the inn in the middle of the night, preferring to roam the streets until dawn rather than to stay in the haunted Eclipse.

THE HYDE TAVERN
(Winchester. Map reference: 60)

Here again is a haunted pub with monastic origins, yet in this case the ghost is not a monk. The oldest pub in Winchester, the Hyde Tavern is believed to have once been part of the Benedictine establishment known as Hyde Abbey. Later it was used by pilgrims who came to pray in Winchester Cathedral.

The activity of the invisible ghost seems like a playful trick until one hears the legend and realises its tragic connotations. The spirit of the pub has manifested herself by slowly drawing blankets off beds so even though the blankets have been carefully tucked in, that sleepers have woken up wondering why they feel cold. According to local tradition the ghost is that of a poor woman who was refused shelter when the inn was a pilgrims' hostel, and as a result died of cold outside.

THE KIMPTON DOWN INN
(Kimpton. Map reference: 87)

A classic case of pub haunting occurred at the Kimpton Down Inn about twenty years ago. It was classic because supernatural manifestations were sparked off by carpenters making alterations to the bar. Apparently the resident spirit disapproved of the renovations and this disapproval was expressed by a burst of poltergeist-type activity. An unseen hand seized beer bottles and shattered them, a mantelpiece was swept clear of ornaments, and glasses and plates of food were overturned. But, as in other cases where inns are concerned, it was not just the work of some mischievous elemental. On several occasions during afternoons or evenings staff members and customers glimpsed a misty female figure.

News of the apparition prompted the memories of some of the older villagers who recalled a grisly legend about a long ago murder at the pub when the wife of a landlord was imprisoned in the cellar and left to die of starvation.

THE ROYAL ANCHOR HOTEL
(Liphook. Map reference: 137)

If ever a hostelry had the right to use the word 'royal' in its name, it must be this delightful hotel. It is said to have started as a hunting lodge used by the ill-fated Edward II. When the House of Plantagenet fell to Henry Tudor it became an inn known as the Blue Anchor which afforded hospitality to Queen Elizabeth I when she broke her journey to Cowdrey Castle.

Her example was later followed by James I, Charles II and Queen Anne. It was George III who was so pleased with the inn that he commanded that its name be changed from the Blue Anchor to The Royal Anchor. William IV – perhaps one of England's most reluctant kings – found the inn very much to his liking. Probably the name was particularly pleasing to him because his happiest years had been spent in the navy. Here the bluff old sailor king felt at ease, spending a lot of time in the kitchen where he ate bread and cheese which he cut with his clasp knife.

The next royal visitors were more decorous – Queen Victoria and Prince Albert.

But not all of the guests were blue-blooded or of the distinction of Samuel Pepys, who noted in his diary for the night of 6 August, 1668, 'Here good honest people'. The Hampshire highwayman Captain Jacques was also a frequenter of the inn. He was particularly feared by travellers on the road running from Petersfield to Liphook. No doubt one of the attractions of the place to a man of his calling was its various secret passages, one of which was believed to run beneath the Square to the cellar of the now demolished Ship Inn.

Captain Jacques probably hoped to escape via this tunnel when agents of the law converged upon the Royal Anchor following a tip-off that he was there. Searching the inn room by room, they burst open the door of a bedroom where they saw the road agent desperately trying to wrench open a secret door in the fireplace which had jammed at the worst possible moment. Behind it was a flight of narrow steps leading down to the secret passages.

The failure of the door cost the highwayman his life. Following a fusillade of pistol shots, he fell dying in the hearth.

Since then there have been occasional reports of a figure wearing a three-cornered hat and an old-fashioned caped riding coat appearing briefly in room 6 where Captain Jacques met his end. He is said to materialise from the fireplace and cross the room to disappear through the closed door – a trick which the fugitive would have found highly useful in life.

THE ROYAL OAK
(Langstone. Map reference: 141)

The Royal Oak at Langstone, the small village opposite Hayling Island, stands on a quay overlooking the Saltings. These are mud flats dissected by channels with vivid green grass growing on the higher banks. From them comes a smell of seaweed that whisks one back to one's childhood days of buckets and spades, shrimping nets and exciting seaside pools.

The haunting of the Royal Oak is the loud sound of a chair being dragged over the stone tiles in the bar. The wife of landlord Peter Spring has often heard it, and so has her married daughter, Penny.

'It is very loud,' Penny told me, 'and just as though you were trying to pull a chair after you across the room. I know of no explanation for it. The other thing we hear is footsteps on the stairs but, again, there is nothing to be seen.'

Apart from the sounds of scraping and footsteps, the occupants of the Royal Oak are sometimes aware of a 'presence'.

'I first knew there was something strange in the Royal Oak when I was a little girl,' Penny added. 'I remember waking up one night with the light being turned on. At first I thought it was my mother coming to see that I was all right. Then I noticed that the door was closed, but as I watched, the door opened, then closed again and the light went out. That always happened when I could see there was nobody there.'

Whatever it is that haunts the Royal Oak, it remains active although its story has long been lost.

The most dramatic haunting happened to Mrs Spring, who said that one night, when her daughter was quite small, she woke up, aware that someone or something was in her bedroom. She explained, 'I thought it was Penny at first when I saw a figure standing by my bed. I asked her what she wanted, and when I got no reply I thought she must be sleep-walking.' She realised she was mistaken when the figure turned and silently glided across the room to vanish into a full-length mirror.

Hereford and Worcester

YE OLDE SEVEN STARS
(Kidderminster. Map reference: 120)

It was a story in a local newspaper which drew attention to the unusual apparition which haunts this pub. According to the report Mrs Freda Holloway stated that she was in the bar when she heard her name called. She turned and saw a woman standing at the end of the bar. Her clothes were white and 'seemed to be the kind worn at the turn of the century'. Then, to Mrs Holloway's consternation, she disappeared.

The ghost was seen several times after that by Mrs Holloway, and her story was backed by the wife of the landlord who confirmed that the spectre had the habit of calling customers by name, and sometimes by nickname. This raises the interesting point as to whether the name was actually said aloud by the ghost, or whether it seemed that way to people of a psychic nature capable of picking up paranormal emanations. Similarly, does a ghost really appear, or is it seen in the mind's eye of the beholder? If it is the latter case it would explain why ghosts are seen by some people and not by others.

After the story about the white lady of Ye Olde Seven Stars had appeared, a reader sent the newspaper a letter saying that his mother had been born on the premises towards the end of the last century, and she too had seen the ghost which she described as wearing a large old fashioned apron. Then it was thought that the manifestation was the result of a tragic death. But there seems to be no explanation as to why the white lady attracts attention to herself by calling out customers' names.

Hertfordshire

THE GEORGE III
(Hoddesdon. Map reference: 71)

The George III was one of the final twelve in the 1982 survey carried out by Teacher's Whisky to find the most authentic haunted pubs of Britain.

The landlord, Rex Gardner, told me that the previous publican was so convinced the place was haunted that when he and his wife were considering taking over the tenancy nine years ago Mrs Gardner asked a vicar to carry out a service of exorcism on the premises.

'Our predecessors told us stories about things jumping about of their own accord,' said Mr Gardner. 'We still have knocks on doors which when you open them you find there is no one there and things drop off walls by themselves. One thing which has intrigued me since I've been here is the behaviour of my dog. He will follow me anywhere, except down the steps into the cellar. Guy Playfair, the expert who was sent by Teacher's, said that the dog's fear of whatever it is in the cellar was pretty convincing.'

THE WHITE HART
(Hemel Hempstead. Map reference: 165)

The White Hart, which goes back to the early part of the 16th century, is haunted by a 'something' which has induced a sensation of sheer terror into certain customers. This zone of fear is situated close to a flight of stairs where it is said a young man was killed when he tried to fight off members of a press gang who wanted to take him away for military service.

It would seem that the terror he experienced in his last moments of life has in some way remained down the years to affect certain persons who are on the right 'psychic wavelength' to receive it. But the haunting has not been confined to this alarming sensation. A ghostly face has been seen to float as though supported by an invisible body and it was said that the features were twisted in an expression of horror.

Humberside

THE FEATHERS
(Pocklington. Map reference: 61)

There is nothing very unusual about The Feathers unless it is the silhouette of a black cat which a previous proprietor fixed high up on the front wall to bring him luck. Yet its yard was once crowded with townsfolk who gazed with fascination at the gallows which had been erected in its yard. The man who stood there with the noose around his neck was a highwayman who had killed a servant girl who had worked at The Feathers, and it was perhaps fitting that he should swing into eternity so close to the scene of the tragedy.

Since that day, 'something supernatural' has haunted the hotel. Its nature is uncertain but an example was given by the landlord who said, 'Not long ago a gentleman booked in. I put him into a room upstairs, Number 7, but when he came to sign the register and I gave him the key, he said: "I'm not staying in that room – not after the terrible experience I had when I was here before."

'It transpired that he had woken up in this room at about two o'clock in the morning. There were no screams or shouts or anything like that, but someone was breathing heavily and someone was obviously trying to pull somebody down the corridor. The guest wondered if it was the fellow next door – perhaps he was having a heart attack – but, for some strange reason, he felt unable to do anything about it. The odd thing was that the man in the next room was also awake, but he stayed in bed, too.

'The guest told me that until someone gave him a call in the morning he dared not get up. When he did, he went next door to see if his neighbour was all right. He was and the two men compared notes. Both had heard the strange sounds for which there was no logical explanation.'

Kent

THE BLACK BULL
(Cliffe. Map reference: 18)

'Ghosts? There are supposed to be hundreds of the so-and-sos,' said landlord John Rawe when I asked him about the phantom footsteps which were reputed to haunt the upper part of his pub. 'But I can't say that I've seen one. It could be because the place was exorcised – twice! – just before we moved in five months ago.

'According to the locals involved the place was heaped up with ghosts and people from the Pentecostal Church in Gravesend came to lay them. The first exorcism didn't clear the place completely so another ceremony was held a fortnight later.

'There has been a pub on this site – though not this building – for hundreds of years, so I suppose things could have accumulated. I've heard that a previous landlord threw himself head first down the well and another hanged himself . . . and there is the sailor who they say they can't exorcise.

'Although I don't believe in ghosts, it does worry me sometimes.'

THE BLACK HORSE
(Pluckley. Map reference: 23)

'I swear the inn is haunted,' declared Peggy Whiting, the landlady of the Black Horse. It was not surprising to hear her say so, for Pluckley, as any villager there will tell you, is the most haunted village in England.

A lot of this haunting is connected with the Dering family who owned the Black Horse before it became an inn 150 years ago. The building itself is between 650 and 680 years old, and most of it is still original. Like many other ghosts in British pubs, its resident spirit takes a puckish delight in making things disappear.

'There is certainly nothing malicious about it,' the landlady declared. 'There is too much of a friendly atmosphere for that.' Her staff bore out what she was saying about the pranks played by the ghost.

Jill, the barmaid, described how she once mislaid a black cardigan while working in the bar.

'I searched everywhere for it and I asked everyone around if they had seen it, but it seemed to have vanished into thin air,' she said. 'Yet two years later, there it was, just as though I had put it down that day. This sort of thing often happens here. Things disappear and then turn up months, or even years, later.' But such a spirit is small beer compared to the rest of the phantoms which inhabit Pluckley.

Mrs Whiting explained that the Dering estate, which used to include the village, was granted to Lord Dering by Charles II for his loyalty during the Civil War.

'He was granted as much land as he could ride his horse around in twenty-four hours,' she said.

I noticed the windows of the Black Horse had a peculiar characteristic, the tops of them were like an inverted U, and I found there was a romantic reason for this. During the Civil War, Dering had a hair's breadth escape from the Roundheads by diving out of such a window. When he came to build his estate he decreed that every window should be shaped like this in memory of his escape. Not only does the Black Horse have these inverted U windows but many of the buildings in Pluckley carry these mementoes of the first lord.

Another ghost vaguely connected with the Black Horse is that of an unfortunate school teacher who committed suicide. From time to time, he is seen in a lane opposite the inn, dangling from one of the trees where he hanged himself.

From villagers I learned of the other phantoms which have given Pluckley its bizarre reputation. Indeed, ghost hunters make a Mecca of the village and even London school teachers bring children down as a special treat. At the annual fair the showing of a film made by the local vicar, depicting the haunted sites of the village, has been one of the most popular events.

'There are so many ghosts here it is hard to say exactly how many there are,' a local resident explained, 'but there must be a couple of dozen.'

These include the shadowy figure of a woman in 20th century dress, sometimes seen in the church; the shade of a soldier who marches through Park Wood; a phantom coach which rumbles through the village at midnight from time to time, and unearthly screams which have been heard since the time when a worker died at the local brickworks as the result of a fall.

The village has a crossroads close to a little stone bridge (where, needless to say, a ghost is sometimes seen on autumn nights in the form of an old gypsy smoking a pipe), and near it is the stump of an oak tree which no doubt brings a delicious thrill of excitement to the school children who come to Pluckley. Here a highwayman was finally run to earth. As he stood with his back to the tree, defending himself to the last, one of his attackers lunged forward with a sword and the blade, running through his body, embedded itself in the bark. It is said that in bright moonlight, this grisly drama is played out again and again by phantom figures.

The most dramatic phenomenon of Pluckley relates to the Dering family. The village church of St Nicholas is said to be haunted by Lady Dering, a woman renowned for her beauty several centuries ago. When she died, her griefstricken husband, frantic at the thought of her beauty returning to dust, had his dead wife dressed in her richest attire with a red rose at her breast. She was placed in three lead coffins, one fitting inside the other rather like the sarcophagi of the famous Tutankhamun. This triple coffin was then enclosed in an oak casket and placed in the family vault beneath the Dering chapel in St Nicholas', where her spectre has been seen walking in the churchyard complete with the flower which was the last gift from her husband.

The church is also famous for strange lights which are seen through a stained glass window by the Dering chapel, and from which mysterious knocking sounds issue.

The churchyard is haunted by another female member of the Dering family, known locally as the Red Lady, an unhappy spirit who is said to be searching among the tombs for a lost baby.

92

THE CHEQUERS
(Smarden. Map reference: 40)

It was after the victory at Waterloo that a soldier, paid off after serving through the Napoleonic Campaign, marched into Smarden and took a room at The Chequers. In the bar the locals hung on his words as he described the Iron Duke and the fighting he had seen under his command. Nor did the locals mind when he bought rounds of drinks, remarking as he paid that there was plenty more where that came from. He explained that he was on his way home where he planned to use his back pay as the capital to go into business on his own behalf.

The affluence of the genial veteran did not go unnoticed by several ruffians and after he had retired full of ale and good humour, they stole into his room and murdered him while he slept.

Today it is believed that the footsteps sometimes heard in the pub are a supernatural echo of the unfortunate soldier. They have been described as going to and fro between two bedrooms – the dividing wall being no obstacle to the invisible presence – and there is something about the uncanny pacing which suggests a soldier on sentry duty.

THE GEORGE INN
(Newington. Map reference: 74)

There is a particularly nasty legend behind the ghost which returns to this six-centuries-old pub. The monk-like figure who has been seen on the premises is said to go back before the Reformation, being the nephew of the Earl of Rochester. He took holy orders but legend tells that his feelings for a nun in a nearby convent brought disaster upon them both.

'I don't know why, but we call the ghost David,' said landlord Peter Martin. 'The story is that he was caught with a nun in what is known as a compromising position, and as a punishment she was walled up alive in a local monastery, now long gone, and he was strangled and thrown down a well in our back garden.

'There is a tradition that a holly tree was planted over the top of the well. In fact we have got a holly tree in our garden between two and three hundred years old which may be a descendant of the one which marked the monk's last resting place.'

Mr Martin says that he has not experienced anything paranormal at the pub himself though the rest of his family have been aware of the monk's haunting.

'A strange thing happened with our four-year-old daughter when we moved into the pub four years ago,' he said. 'She drew a picture of a person who she said came to visit her every night. We did not think anything of it at the time, but she continued to draw pictures of a person who looked as though he was wearing a hood. We heard rumours of the pub being haunted but we didn't want to worry her so we told her to think of it as a friend who was just coming to say goodnight.'

THE KING'S HEAD
(Grafty Green. Map reference: 91)

A phantom coach and the ghost of a smuggler are the supernatural manifestations which have been associated with the King's Head. The area surrounding the village of Grafty Green was once notorious for its bands of smugglers, one of which engaged in a running fight with the excisemen but they were captured at Chilston. As they were led away manacled, they found one of their leaders, the notorious Dover Bill, was not with them. They next saw him when they were in the dock and he was giving evidence against them. Soon afterwards they were hanged publicly at Peneden Heath.

After the hanging none of the informer's friends in Grafty Green would speak to him, and if he ventured to greet a neighbour the villager would look through him as though he did not exist. Drinks were refused him at the King's Head.

Indeed Dover Bill was treated as though he was a ghost long before he became one. No one would employ him and he found it difficult to get food. He died miserable and penniless. It is said his ghost has returned to the King's Head where in happier days he used to enjoy his leisure hours.

Landlord Richard Jackson said that to his knowledge the

ghost of Dover Bill has not walked in the King's Head recently but the other phantom connected with the inn is still active, although it is heard more frequently than it is seen.

In coaching days, a coach and four once set off from the King's Head bound for Lenham late at night. After the driver had whipped up his horses something made them take fright and bolt and, as the swaying vehicle reached the bend at the nearby church, the frenzied beasts plunged to the right instead of taking the left fork. Local legend suggests it was the shade of Dover Bill which terrified the team.

They hurtled down a drive into the old rectory and crashed into a tree. The horses were killed and the coach smashed to matchwood. The passengers perished inside the ghastly shambles – while the unfortunate coachman was flung from his seat and decapitated.

'From time to time villagers report having heard the sound of the runaway horses and the noise of the terrible impact,' said Mr Jackson. 'One man I know quite well told me about it. He is a local gardener and when walking home from the pub late one night he passed the old rectory and suddenly heard the most blood-chilling sounds.

'It was the noise made by horses in their death throes mingled with the dying screams of passengers in the wrecked coach. The man was completely shaken by his experience and said that he had never heard anything so horrible in all his life.'

THE RED LION
(Wingham. Map reference: 131)

To the connoisseur of historic old inns the Red Lion is well worth a visit. The foundations were laid in 1286 when it formed part of a monastic establishment, after the Dissolution it became a private house, and as an inn it was the venue for the local Court of Petty Sessions from 1703 to 1886. It was also used as the headquarters of the village fire brigade in the days when the pumping engine was drawn by horses. In the stables at the back of the inn you can still see their stalls, while the names painted above them are simple memorials to 'Snips' and his team mates.

Old books on inns suggest that the Red Lion was haunted though references to the supernatural trail off in modern times. According to a villager who has spent all his life in Wingham the phantom connected with the pub was that of a suicide.

'He used to be seen walking past a wall of the Red Lion at midnight,' he explained. 'He was quite real-looking, but suddenly he would vanish into thin air.'

THE RINGLESTONE TAVERN
(Harrietsham. Map reference: 135)

'Drop the other shoe!' used to be a line guaranteed to bring laughter in a comedy sketch whether in the theatre or on television. The basic plot is that the comedian is in a flat or boarding-house room with his girl friend, who he is endeavouring to woo into an amorous situation. She is starting to respond when the proceedings are interrupted by a tipsy neighbour clumping upstairs to the room above. The sound of footsteps through the ceiling indicates his progress towards bed while the two characters below gaze upwards, waiting for the silence which will allow them to continue. And then, just as they settle back on the sofa, the neighbour throws down *one* shoe . . . and the rest of the sketch is their frustration waiting for the other shoe to drop.

The ghost at the three-centuries-old Ringlestone Tavern could easily have been a comic from the old music hall days. Although he has not been seen, he has made people acutely aware of his presence by very loud footfalls. These were heard on the cellar stairs late at night. From their sound the progress of the ghost could be traced to the top step where he halted, and then a few seconds later dropped a single shoe.

One theory is that in life he was about to creep about the tavern in stockinged feet on some nefarious activity when he was caught by the landlord.

THE SHIPWRIGHT'S ARMS
(Faversham. Map reference: 148)

For three hundred years the Shipwright's Arms has looked over a desolate landscape of marsh and creeks. When the wind sweeps in from the sea, sending ripples across the surrounding reeds and moaning eerily round its clapboard walls, it could be a film set for an adventure story about Dr Syn-type smugglers.

It would be remarkable if such an atmospheric pub was not haunted and, true to form, its ghost is that of a tough-looking skipper in an old fashioned reefer jacket. He has been seen by customers and past landlords of the pub. One regular from the boatyard which stands next door reported how a 'seafaring' man came into the bar when he was having a drink by himself. He took hardly any notice of the stranger until he disappeared.

The wife of a previous licensee has described seeing his figure standing at the bottom of her bed before fading away. This manifestation occurred three nights running. An old marshland tale suggests that the captain came across the marsh after his ship was wrecked one night. He managed to reach the door of the Shipwright's Arms before collapsing, and in the morning he was found dead from cold and exhaustion.

THE WALNUT TREE
(Aldington. Map reference: 159)

This inn was once the base of the notorious Aldington Gang which, at the beginning of the last century, controlled a massive smuggling operation on the Romney Marsh. Today it is a well-drained area used for sheep-grazing, but then it was a wild swampy stretch ideal for the landing of contraband brandy and tobacco. The inhabitants of such smuggling villages as Dymchurch would 'watch the wall . . . while the gentlemen passed by' – as Kipling put it – especially if the gentlemen happened to be members of the feared Aldington Gang.

George Ransley, the leader of the smugglers, chose the Walnut Tree as it was strategically placed to give him a view across the marsh. From a window at the rear of the building he answered lantern signals from his men on the coast by displaying a light which would guide them to the inn after their illegal cargoes had been run ashore.

It was the gang's reputation for violence which kept freelance freetraders off its territory, and it was this violence which led to the haunting of the Walnut Tree. An occupational hazard of smugglers in the days of sail was boredom – of having to wait around for favourable tides and weather conditions to allow the French craft to slip into English waters with their contraband. Members of the Aldington Gang, often waiting for nights on end, killed time by playing cards and drinking the spirits which they imported.

After midnight on one such night a quarrel flared up over the card table, knives flashed into the open and a second later one of the smugglers was stabbed to death. The killing quickly sobered the gang and the murderer was told to dispose of his victim's body immediately so that no suspicions would be aroused which might bring the excise down upon them. He carried the corpse outside to a well situated close to the inn and dropped it down the deep shaft.

The haunting which followed was very similar to that of The Caxton Gibbet, and takes place in the early hours when disembodied sounds are heard of someone moving slowly to the old well as though carrying a heavy burden . . .

THE WHITE HORSE
(Chilham. Map reference: 167)

One of the most punctual phantoms on record must be the vicar who, when he materialises at the White Horse, does so at exactly 10.10 am. Guests entering the pub at that time have greeted him in the belief that the benign clerical gentleman, in a black cassock and with his back to the fireplace, was a living person. It was only when he vanished before their eyes that they knew that they had just had an encounter of the supernatural kind.

In life the ghost was the Reverend Sampson Hieron, the noncomformist vicar of the village three centuries ago, and the reason he returns to the White Horse is that, in the 17th century, it was not an inn but a house which for some time was his home. It seems he was very happy here, and it must have been a great sadness to him when he was forced to leave because of his nonconformist views. Perhaps that is why he enjoys revisiting it in these more liberal days.

Lancashire

THE BRIDGE HOUSE
(Hapton. Map reference: 28)

For many people waterside pubs hold a special fascination
whether they overlook the sea, lakes or rivers, and some of the
most pleasant I have discovered are those dreaming beside
canals where once narrow-boat men tied up for a few pints and
a gossip. Sadly there are few working boats left. Their places
are taken on the inland waterways by weekend cruisers, but the
pubs at least retain an atmosphere of a more leisurely era.

Such a pub is The Bridge House which stands on the bank of
the Leeds and Liverpool Canal. It was once an important
stopping place for canal traffic and had a special stable for the
great horses which were once a familiar sight on the country's
towpaths. Sometimes this building was used as a temporary
morgue for bodies of the drowned, and perhaps it was because
of this that the pub became haunted.

The spectre which has been reported by a succession of
landlords over the years is that of a young girl who ended her
life by throwing herself from the nearby bridge into the canal.
She may have worked at the pub, or had some close connection
with it, because she has always been glimpsed on steps which
lead to the pantry.

DUNKENHALGH HOTEL
(Clayton-le-Moors. Map reference: 59)

The story of the tragic phantom associated with the Dunkenhalgh Hotel would have made an ideal subject for a Victorian
sentimental ballad – or a Victorian melodrama. A tale of
seemingly betrayed love, it was set in the early 18th century
when the hotel was then the family home of the Walmesleys

which, on the marriage of Katherine Walmesley, passed to her husband Robert Petre. When the couple had several young children a French governess named Lucette was engaged to look after them.

She was soon a favourite of the children, especially when she took them for long walks in the vast grounds of Dunkenhalgh Park. The excursion they found most enjoyable was to the stone bridge that spanned a river flowing through the estate. The girl was equally popular with other members of the family, and all went well until one Christmas when she met, and fell in love with, a young army officer on leave from a Continental campaign. Before rejoining his regiment he promised the trusting Lucette that he would marry her when he returned in spring.

When that time came Lucette admitted to the Petres that she was carrying his child and she feared that he had abandoned her. They tried to reassure her, saying that as a scion of a Dunkenhalgh family he was a soul of honour but with war in Europe he was unlikely to be able to come back to England when he wished.

Lucette was treated with true kindness by the Petres, but she could not help being affected by the household servants who did not share their master and mistress' compassion for the 'foreigner'. As the weeks went by and her condition became more and more obvious, the girl could not bear the thought of them sneering behind her back. Their whispers preyed on her nerves, and one day in June she left the house to escape them, following the path to the old bridge along which she had brought the Petre children in happier days.

The river was running high from a recent rainstorm and as she gazed at the foam-flecked water from the mossy parapet she became convinced that she would never see her lover again. The thought of life without him, and of bearing what was then known as a 'love child', was too much for the distraught governess, and she leapt into the torrent.

When Lucette's young officer returned to Dunkenhalgh a week later, eager to wed his French sweetheart, the Petres broke the news of her suicide to him and said how when her body had been found among the rushes, they had wrapped her in a shroud and given her a decent burial.

Soon afterwards there was another arrival at Dunkenhalgh; the brother of Lucette came to visit his sister and when he learned of her fate he challenged the young officer to a duel for the 'shame' and tragedy he had brought upon her. When the two met early one morning the encounter was short, the Frenchman avenging his sister with a mortal sword thrust.

Since then – usually at Christmas – the ghost of poor Lucette has been seen close to the bridge where she took her life. Wearing the shroud in which she was wrapped when her body was discovered, she appears to glide along the path by the river and then fades away as she approaches the scene of her death.

THE MIDLAND HOTEL
(Morecambe. Map reference: 105)

This hotel, named after the Midland Railway Company which built it, has a phantom who, according to the folklore which has grown up around him, has been the reason for the hurried resignation of several porters when they encountered it.

A bizarre aspect of this spirit, who has been described as a figure with misty edges, is that he appears to be able to operate the hotel lift. On one such occasion a member of the night staff saw a shape materialise out of a door behind which steps lead down to the cellar. The spectre then appeared to float across the hall towards the lift. Here the doors opened to admit him, then closed and the cage ascended to an upper floor.

The Midland Hotel apparition may be the ghost of an airman who died during World War II when the premises were converted into a hospital for officers of the RAF. The cellar, from whence the ghost appears, was used as a mortuary.

THE NEW INN
(Foulridge. Map reference: 108)

A cross glowing on the ceiling of a small back bedroom was the curious manifestation which made the New Inn famous among the ghost-hunting fraternity at the beginning of this century. Once night fell and darkness filled the room the luminous symbol would appear, though no satisfactory explanation for it was ever found. Perhaps in some mysterious way it was connected with the old Quakers' cemetery nearby. When it became neglected, tombstones were removed from it to use as building material in a wall adjoining the pub.

Apart from the cross, the New Inn has a ghost which announces its presence by knocking at the door of the landlord's bedroom with invisible knuckles, or by the sound of footsteps along the passages. Some think the invisible prowler is the spirit of a cavalier who was killed here during the Civil War.

One local legend relating to that time is that the name of the village came about when Cromwell arrived there with his army during a storm. Looking across the valley to Pendle Hill, he remarked to his lieutenants, 'This is a foul ridge on which to fight a battle, we'll fight down there.'

THE OLD ORIGINAL INN
(Scouthead. Map reference: 112)

Eliza Jane was a nineteen-year-old servant girl who drowned herself in 1906 after being chastised for her bad drinking habits. Seventy years later her ghost was known as the haunter of the Old Original Inn to which she used to come unobtrusively to buy her liquor.

'I have been seeing the ghost over five years,' landlady Vera Manner told the *Oldham Evening Chronicle* in November, 1978. 'When I first saw it I didn't tell anyone because I thought they would think that I was going off my rocker. All I see is a shape. It is very quick and moves faster than a human being.'

Mrs Manner never mentioned the apparition to her children in case they were alarmed, but her son Nicholas, aged thirteen, described to her exactly what she had seen.

'The ghost is always crossing the pub in the same area,' she said. 'In those days the set-up was different and it was the route through the back door of a shop to the room which served as a pub. If Eliza was being discouraged from drinking she would use the path from the farm where she worked by the back door. From the sound of things this was probably the only place where she was happy.'

THE PUNCH BOWL
(Hurst Green. Map reference: 126)

For over a century a restless ghost plagued this inn causing bottles to jump from shelves and disturbing sleepers with eerie sounds. Forty years ago a priest was invited to perform an exorcism there to release the earthbound spirit, but the ceremony was only partially successful. The supernatural activity lessened but did not cease altogether, and today there are reports of a moaning sound being heard which has no normal explanation.

The blame for this is put on Ned King, a young highwayman who brought notoriety to the Punch Bowl when he had a shoot-out with the militia there. During his career as a road agent he used the inn as a base, and his favourite stratagem was to hide in the hayloft where he could watch out for travellers who looked wealthy enough to rob. Once the victim went off down the road in his coach King would ride over the fields and be waiting to greet him at a suitable bend with the traditional 'Stand and deliver!'

Finally he was cornered in the hayloft where he blazed away at members of the militia until his supply of powder and ball ran out and he surrendered. Soon afterwards he was hanged at the appropriately named Gallows Lane not far from the Punch Bowl where once he had been toasted as King of the Road.

THE RING O' BELLS
(Middleton. Map reference: 134)

This ancient pub, the oldest building in Middleton, is famous for the ghost of a cavalier with a sorrowful expression. Carrying a sword, and dressed in the height of royalist fashion, he has been seen frequently in the pub and is thought to be the victim of Parliamentarian troops who killed him in a nearby church.

A link with the legend was discovered a few years ago when some flagstones were raised in the cellar and bones and weapons from the time of the Civil War were found. Perhaps they were the bones of the slain cavalier who for some long forgotten reason had been buried in the Ring o' Bells' cellar. Another aspect of the haunting is the sound of mysterious footsteps pacing in the cellar where the find was made.

SMACKWATER JACK'S
(Burnley. Map reference: 150)

The delightfully named Smackwater Jack's establishment is a comparative newcomer to the licensed trade, being a wine bar which was opened six years ago – yet it can boast an aural phenomenon along with the best of our haunted pubs.

The ghost was first heard when the old warehouse was being converted into the Edwardian-inspired bar. One evening one of the men behind the venture was startled to hear the sound of loud footsteps echoing from an old stairway. The builders had knocked off for the day, so he went to investigate and found the stairwell, and the rest of the premises, completely deserted.

From then on disembodied footsteps have been heard frequently, and customers with knowledge of local history are inclined to the belief that they are those of a young man who died while working in the warehouse during Victorian times.

THE SUN INN
(Chipping. Map reference: 154)

Lizzie Dean is the spectre who haunts this pub where 130 years ago she worked as a serving maid. Tragedy came when she was jilted – some say her lover never arrived at the church on the day they were to be married – and she took her life. The landlord of the pub has seen her misty figure on several occasions, and once she was seen to walk into the main bar and then vanish through a seemingly solid wall. She was described as wearing a long dress and had her hair piled up on her head.

Later it was found that the wall was not quite as solid as it appeared. The landlord decided that a serving hatch there would be a useful innovation, and when the builders began work they found that there was a sealed-up door hidden in the plaster and masonry – a door through which Lizzie Dean would have passed many times a day when she went to and from the pub's kitchen.

Leicestershire

THE BELPER ARMS
(Newton Burgoland. Map reference: 15)

Visitors to this pub have sometimes had a shock when they stood on the spot where an old spiral staircase used to be. Long ago something out of the ordinary or highly dramatic must have happened on those stairs because a psychic 'something' has lingered down the years. It manifests itself by the temperature suddenly plunging so that coming from the warm bar the visitor suddenly finds him or herself shuddering with cold – and what understandably increases the shuddering is the sensation of an invisible hand covering the face. Unfortunately there is no known explanation for the phenomenon.

THE BLUEBELL INN
(Belmersthorpe. Map reference: 27)

There is a charming touch of folklore connected with the haunting of this old inn. Dorothy Bradbury, wife of the landlord, explained, 'Lady Godiva lived in a castle at the top of what is now Castle Ride. She got married as a young girl to Earl Leofric who had said to her, "I'll give you this little hamlet as a wedding present. What would you like to call it?" She said, "Bells from the church, and mist from the river over the meadows." And from this was made up the name of the village . . . Bell-mist-thorpe.'

Having got her village, Lady Godiva built a small monastery there, and this in turn became the site of the Bluebell Inn.

'The inn was said to be haunted by the ghost of a hunchback,' Mrs Bradbury continued. 'In the days when this was a monastery he used to bring messages from the castle. I have never seen him but the local story is that on foggy nights you could hear him dragging his feet on the gravel. When he was seen he used to vanish at the inn well.'

Although Mrs Bradbury has not encountered this phantom messenger, she did have one alarming experience at the pub.

'It was late one night, or – I should say – early one morning,' she explained. 'We had some old friends round the bar and were drinking coffee. Suddenly the door appeared to be open and I saw a tall dark figure in the room. In that moment I thought it was a policeman checking up, and I jumped off my stool in surprise.' The guests saw the figure as well as it quickly crossed the room and vanished down a passage. Mrs Bradbury's husband went after it to see who it was, but no trace of an intruder could be found, and the pub was securely locked.

'Afterwards I realised that what I first thought was a policeman in a long black mac could have been a monk in his robe,' said Mrs Bradbury.

She added that the reason why the hunchback may not visit the Bluebell any more was that the well he had always been associated with was no more.

'We filled it in,' she said. 'Now the gents' loo is on top of it.'

Lincolnshire

THE SUN
(Saxilby. Map reference: 153)

At the beginning of the last century The Sun, which overlooks
the Fossdyke Canal, was the subject of one of the most
extraordinary pub hauntings ever recorded. The events which
led up to it began on 3 November, 1805, when Thomas Otter
was married much against his will. At dusk on the same day a
casual labourer named John Dunkerly, after drinking in The
Sun, began walking back to his own village of Doddington
which lay about five miles away. Nearing a spot known as
Drisney Nook he met three acquaintances, one of whom said,
'You'll have company, John. Tom Otter and his new wife are
up the lane.' The others laughed, aware that Dunkerly had the
reputation for being a Peeping Tom.

By now darkness had fallen and the labourer, whose
reputation was well deserved, decided to shadow the
newly-married couple in the hope of being able to spy upon
some amorous activity. Creeping up behind them, he heard
Tom Otter say to his wife: 'Sit down, you can rest here.'

Hoping this was the prelude to love-making, Dunkerly
climbed into a field through a hedge, and crawled behind it to
where Mrs Otter was resting on a bank. If Dunkerly had
expected to witness some passionate display, he was in for a
shock. Tom Otter left his wife, climbed into the hedge within a
few paces of the crouching on-looker, and uprooted a heavy
stake.

'The moon shined on his face at the time and his eyes
frightened me, there was such a fiery look in them, like a cat's
eyes in the dark, and I heard him say to himself, "That will
finish my bloody wedding!" ' Dunkerly said in evidence later.

'Then he climbed down to where she was sitting with her
head hanging down, and he swung the hedgestake with both

hands and hit her a clout on the head. She gave one scream and called on God for mercy, then tumbled over with her head on the ground. He hit her again as she lay on the grass, and that time the knock sounded as though he had hit a turnip. I saw her arms and legs all of a-quiver like for a while and then she was still as a cobblestone. I think I went off in a faint.

'When I came round again, the hedgestake he had murdered her with lay close beside me. I took it up and my hand was covered with red, and my smock sleeve dabbled with it. Then I thought if they found me in that state they'd take me for the murderer and hang me, so for days I wandered about. I don't know how long, working on roads and getting a job as how I could. I came back to Doddington on the 20th of March.'

Soon after the murder, the body of Mrs Otter was found. Her husband was arrested at The Sun when an alert constable noticed a dried bloodstain on his clothes. Here, too, the body of the unfortunate bride was brought for the inquest. As it was carried in, blood dripped on to the threshold. When the servants were told to clean it up, they superstitiously refused, stating they would rather leave their jobs than touch the blood of a murder victim. Four months later the stains were still to be seen.

Thomas Otter was executed at Lincoln, after which his body was taken down so it could be hung in irons from a gibbet at Drisney Nook as the usual warning to other violent persons.

Odd things began to happen when the body was transported to where the demonstration gallows and its grisly equipment had been made ready six days after the execution. A moment after the wagon bearing the decomposing body had rumbled across Saxilby bridge, the structure broke and dropped twenty spectators into the water.

When the corpse had been riveted into its irons and was being hauled into position, the crossbar broke and the body, irons and all, fell sickeningly upon the team of men hauling the rope. Among them was John Dunkerly. The beam was repaired and, as the body was once more hauled up, Dunkerly remarked, 'Well, he won't come down any more!' At this the corpse of Tom Otter did come down, crashing heavily on to the Peeping Tom.

The landlord of the Sun acquired the fatal hedgestake and

exhibited it in the bar of his inn in order to attract custom. In those days, when the country population had little to entertain them, the sight of the morbid relic in the bar was enough to put the yokels into great good humour.

On the anniversary of the murder it was found that the stake had vanished, and a little while later a farmer located it lying behind the hedge at Drisney Nook where the murder had been committed. The same thing happened the following year and finally the landlord of The Sun, tiring of the stake's supernatural disappearances, gave it to the landlord of an inn at nearby Torksey, who had long wanted it to increase his own bar trade.

Fearing the trophy might be removed by some of his more unruly customers, he had it clamped to the wall of the bar with three iron hasps, but on the following 4 November the hasps were mysteriously torn from the wall and the stake had vanished.

As before, it was found in the field at Drisney Nook. That was enough for the Torksey landlord, and he passed it on to the Peewit Inn whose landlord commissioned the blacksmith of Saxilby – the same man who had constructed the suit of chains for Otter's body – to make cast-iron staples to secure it, but on the next anniversary both the staples and stake vanished. The latter was recovered in the usual place, and this time it was bolted to the wall with half-a-dozen clamps.

The next November, a party of villagers planned to stay the night at the inn and keep watch. With some misgivings they sat in the darkened bar but, no doubt having over-fortified themselves with brandy, dropped off to sleep. When they rubbed their eyes in the morning and looked at the wall on which the stake had been bolted, they saw the clamps had been torn out and the crude weapon had once again disappeared.

The mysterious activities of the hedgestake had now become too much for everybody and, in order to calm the locals, the Bishop of Lincoln ordered it to be removed from the inn and burned under the walls of Lincoln Cathedral.

As far as the public were concerned this was the end of the puzzling affair, but, during his last illness, John Dunkerly told a visiting clergyman how the stake came to be found so regularly at Drisney Nook. The parson passed the account on to a

Victorian author who recorded the words for posterity.

'It was the very night of the murder, exactly a twelve-month afterwards, that I felt doley-like, so I went to bed about dusk hours, and what I'm trying to tell you is as true as I'm a dying man,' the expiring voyeur confessed. 'I couldn't sleep, and while I was like that, all of a sudden Tom Otter stood in front of me in his chains, and says: "It's time, come along." And I had to go with him. And he says: "Fetch it – make haste." And I broke into The Sun, at Saxilby, and fetched the hedgestake that he had murdered her with from off the nail where it was hanging up, and when I got outside the door they were both waiting for me, and we all three went over Saxilby bridge together.

'She was walking behind and carrying a paper box in one hand and a pair of pattens' [these were overshoes for keeping shoes out of the mud] 'in the other. She was wearing the light blue gown she had on that very night the year before. He had on the same light velveteen jacket and breeches that he had on when he came through the hedge and tore up the stake that I was carrying then. It was a kind of mist we seemed to be walking in. We turned down Drisney Nook Lane, and reached the same spot we reached before, and he used the very same words, and said, "Sit down. You can rest here." And she sat down with her head drooping on her breast, like before, and he came up to me, with his eyes more fiery than they was before-time, and says, "Now then, quick."

'And somehow I threw up the hedgestake with both hands and murdered her just the way he did twelve months before. I give her one clout when she was sitting down, and another when she'd fallen over. And every third of November for years, no matter where I might be, the same low-doley feeling came over me, and Tom Otter would come to me in his chains and say: "Now then, it's time," and I had to go and fetch the hedgestake from wherever it might be, and do the same murdering over again, and twice when it was fastened up with staples he came and helped me pull, and said, "You pulled hard enough when you helped to gibbet me!"

'For years this went on, and the hedgestake was always found in the stubble field next morning where I'd thrown it like he did, and when I'd find myself walking back home I'd be all wet with sweat.

'I had no peace until that stake was burnt in the Minster yard. After that was done they never came to fetch me to go with them to murder her no more.'

London Area

THE ASYLUM
(Peckham. Map reference: 8)

'One night, after we had cleared up, I was playing crib with the barman when the keg tap was turned on of its own accord,' said landlord Len Moore. 'At various times the gas cylinders in the cellar have been turned off although there has been no one down there. In the bar lids have been seen to rise off ice buckets by themselves and then drop into place again. We were warned about the ghost when we first came here but we took no notice until these odd things began happening.'

The Asylum – the only pub with this name in England – was one of the twelve chosen by Teacher's as most worthy of investigation, and in this case the well-known ghost hunters Guy Playfair and Maurice Grosse visited The Asylum in search of paranormal happenings.

'Mr Grosse told me that the pub has a ghost and a poltergeist,' said Mr. Moore. 'He said the vibrations of both were here when he came.

'We heard that the ghost was that of an old lady dressed in grey and with her hair in a bun. One night my five-year-old daughter told us that her elder sister had come briefly into her bedroom dressed in grey. The curious thing was that my other daughter wasn't home at the time.'

THE CAULIFLOWER
(Ilford. Map reference: 37)

Communication with a pub ghost came about when the Essex Healers' Association held their annual dinner at The Cauliflower. For some time landlord Deryck Jones and his wife Sue had been worried by mysterious happenings in the cellar, and

Sue took the opportunity to enlist the help of the healers. She explained how some mysterious force flung beer crates and beer cylinders about the floor, how gas taps were turned off when there was no one there and how at times the place was mysteriously flooded.

The spiritualist medium Florence Thompson undertook to exorcise the restless spirit and with her colleagues she performed a ceremony of exorcism in the cellar. It was thought that the phenomena were the result of some bygone person being angry at having his hiding place there sealed up. But Mrs Thompson was dissatisfied with this attempt and returned later on. This time she claimed to have established communication with the ghost who she named as 'Kathy'.

According to the medium, Kathy had been involved with a gang of robbers in the 18th century. Finally, when being pursued by officers of the law, they hid in a large sluice which Mrs Thompson thought had been located close to The Cauliflower. While the gang were in it the sluice gate was opened and the fugitives drowned.

'That's why poor Kathy kept turning the cellar taps off,' Mrs Thompson was reported as saying in the *Publican* of 13 December, 1979. 'She thought that by doing this she would save her friends from drowning. But I managed to bring back one of the gang, a great pal of hers known as "Titch". He talked to Kathy and persuaded her to join him along with the others.'

Deryck Jones reported that following the seance The Cauliflower had been free from disturbances.

THE CROWN AND HORSES
(Enfield. Map reference: 49)

'At first when the door started banging I thought it was warped,' Sue Williamson, wife of the pub's landlord, told the *Enfield Gazette* in 1975. She went on to explain that in fact it was a ghost which slammed the door a dozen times a night. Although the mysterious resident has been reported in other parts of the premises, it does seem to prefer the cellar as its base.

'Our dog which usually follows us everywhere will never even attempt to go down into the cellar,' Mrs Williamson said. Her husband Ray was reported as fleeing upstairs from it when he encountered an inexplicable temperature drop.

In the early part of the last century two murders were committed at the Crown and Horses – in 1816 a gruesome discovery was made at the nearby well when the body of the landlord John Draper was found pushed down it, and sixteen years later a seaman named Benjamin Danby was murdered on the premises. Some believe that this long ago violence could have left a psychic echo which is responsible for the phenomena at the pub. Yet those who have glimpsed the ghost describe it as a 'little old lady'.

One of the regulars at the Crown and Horses who saw the apparition was Brian Bullock. One day he was outside the pub, waiting for a previous landlord to return, when he saw the silhouette of the ghost pass a window. When the landlord came and heard about Mr Bullock's experience he was puzzled because there was no one on the premises which he had securely locked. A search from cellar to attic was carried out but no trace of a human intruder was found.

Other mysterious happenings at the pub have included the ringing of the bell above the bar which is used to herald drinking up time. What worried the customers who saw the bell's wildly swinging chain was that the invisible force which tugged it was trying to clear the bar while there was still enough legal time for a couple of pints.

THE DUKE OF NORTHUMBERLAND
(Isleworth. Map reference: 8)

When landlord Alan Pounds moved from the Duke of Northumberland in May, 1979, he told the *Evening Mail*, 'I'm not one to believe in ghosts, but I find there are things which have happened here which I just can't explain. When you see a light switch go off and on of its own accord, then you start to worry.'

Other things which worried this ex-CID officer were the sound of disembodied footsteps and a force which caused glasses to fall from a shelf in the bar. At times the effect of this force was frightening.

'My mother, who was sitting with one of our bar staff, saw an ashtray move from one side of the table to the other,' said Mr Pounds. His wife Sonya was the object of the poltergeist's most spectacular tricks. One day she was on her own in the pub when a heavy door slammed in her face as she was about to go through the doorway. Worse was a flying bucket.

'I was cooking in the kitchen,' she said, 'when a bucket just flew above my head, right across the room.'

THE GRENADIER
(Wilton Row. Map reference: 8)

London's most famous haunted inn is The Grenadier, a fashionable pub which stands in Wilton Row – a private road belonging to the Grosvenor Estate – just off Wilton Crescent near Hyde Park Corner. Inside, its 300-year-old walls are decorated with press cuttings from newspapers and magazines from all over the world. One journal describes The Grenadier as the 'secret rendezvous of the English gentry', but most of the cuttings relate to the ghost which traditionally haunts the inn during September.

At the beginning of the last century the inn was appropriately called The Guardsman, as it was close to the parade ground used by Wellington's troops. The Duke and his officers used it as their mess and as a place to gamble. Later, the name was changed to its present one after there was an outburst of public criticism over George IV's using it as his local.

According to The Grenadier's legend, a young officer was caught cheating during a game of cards. His brother officers were so outraged they determined to teach him a lesson he would never forget. His grenadier's tunic was torn off and he was flogged until his body was raw.

In those days, the rank and file of the army were used to field punishment, but officers and gentlemen were not made of such stern stuff. The young grenadier reeled away from his tormentors when his punishment was over, stumbled blindly down the stairs into the cellar and died.

Since then various landlords have experienced psychic disturbances at the inn on the anniversary month of the cardsharp's death. Dogs – those faithful barometers of ghostly climate – show symptoms of fear, strange shadows not cast by any visible being are seen on the stairs and on the landing, while customers have sworn to seeing the ghostly shape of a soldier in an old-fashioned uniform.

THE KING'S ARMS
(Peckham Rye. Map reference: 8)

One of the most modern pub hauntings must be that at the King's Arms which stands in Peckham Rye in South London. Here many people have sworn to hearing the ghostly voices of a number of Blitz victims. In 1940 a German bomb scored a direct hit on the pub, killing a number of customers who were sheltering in the cellar. Now a modern glass-fronted pub stands on the site, with Riviera-style sun umbrellas making splashes of colour on the pavement outside on summer days.

'There has been a King's Arms in Peckham Rye for three centuries,' said the landlord, Peter Walsh. 'When they were excavating to build the present one, they found the bones of an *Ichthyosaurus platadon* which was a huge sort of reptile which dates back 200 million years. The skeleton is now in the British Museum.

'As far as the ghosts are concerned, I cannot say I have experienced anything myself, but my daughter-in-law swears she saw the figure of a woman who is thought to have been one of the people killed here during the war,' he said.

The same figure was glimpsed in the restaurant one morning by Pat Lawless, one of the barmen at the King's Arms. He described her as being dressed in old-fashioned clothes. As he watched her she disappeared before his eyes.

It is in the cellar where most of the supernatural activity takes place. An ex-barman, Gary Hallet, has been reported in the press as saying, 'I was down in the cellars one night when I heard voices singing along to a piano. They were singing old songs, like you might hear down the Old Kent Road years ago. I was scared out of my wits and dashed upstairs as fast as I could.'

His story has been corroborated by neighbours of the King's Arms who say they have heard old war-time songs echoing from the pub's cellar late at night. A favourite with the mysterious singers is 'Lili Marlene'.

THE KING'S CELLARS
(Croydon. Map reference: 8)

One of the most curious cases mentioned in Colin Wilson's book *Poltergeist!* concerns the King's Cellars where the paranormal activity created such tension that 'in the twelve years it had been open, it had wrecked the marriages of about a dozen couples'. This activity included glasses moving through the air as though carried by invisible hands, bottles leaping off shelves by themselves and smashing on the floor, the pub's tills jamming at identical moments and wild changes in temperature.

Colin Wilson, who investigated the pub, wrote how one of its managers, Mike Delaney, became aware of the poltergeist activity: 'He had been sent there by the brewery to act as a stopgap until another manager could be found – he was the brewery's "trouble shooter", who went to pubs that were having problems. When he arrived, he knew nothing about the place, and certainly did not believe in ghosts or poltergeists. On the fifth night, he stayed late to examine and balance the books. And since it was a lock-up pub, he decided to stay there overnight in a sleeping bag. After working at the books, he lay down in the sleeping bag on a padded seat. The place seemed unusually cold – far colder than it should have been. And as he closed his eyes, he heard the sound – a rattle of glasses. He sat up, then went over to the bar. All the glasses on the top shelf were vibrating, as if a juggernaut lorry was going past. But there was no juggernaut; all was silent. The place was so icy that he decided to go upstairs and sleep in the office. The next morning he went back to the hotel where he was staying for a shower, locking the pub behind him. When he returned to the downstairs bar, he was surprised to find it covered in broken glass. The row of glasses that had been vibrating had been swept all over the floor. To do this, three dozen glasses had had to cross the bar . . .

118

'Mike now had no doubt that the place was "haunted", but this did not bother him unduly. He said: "I love this place, and I intend to stay." After years of moving from pub to pub, he had found one he liked. A poltergeist was a nuisance, but it did no real harm – except for scaring the staff. It had swept a whole row of beer bottles off the upstairs bar one day, smashing them all. One warm evening, it had made the downstairs bar so cold that two huge fan heaters had no effect, and Mike was forced to close it down . . . One day, with customers in the bar, flames suddenly crept up the wall – with an oddly bright light – and across the ceiling, then they extinguished themselves. The likeliest explanation seemed to be some odd electrical fault; but neither the fire-prevention officer nor the electricity board could find anything wrong.'

A few weeks after Colin Wilson visited the King's Cellars the manager decided that he could no longer stand the strain caused by the poltergeist. One evening he suddenly realised that if he stayed on he would have a nervous breakdown. In admission of defeat he went down into the pub's cellar and said aloud, 'You've beaten me. I'm going.' As though in response, the cellar became icy cold within an instant.

The next manager, who also did not believe in ghosts when he took over, only remained at the King's Cellars for two months.

There are several unusual aspects of the paranormal activity in the pub. Such violent manifestations are usually focussed on some individual; in this case the activity has gone on for years with frequent changes of personnel. Colin Wilson wrote: 'The likeliest theory, then, is that we are dealing with some mischievous entity of the elemental type, which draws some of its energy from human beings, and some from the site itself.'

Many of the hauntings in this book have an element of poltergeist phenomena about them, and for those who are interested in this type of paranormal behaviour I suggest they read Colin Wilson's *Poltergeist!* which is a fascinating collection of case histories from which he draws his own conclusions, making it the definitive work on what he terms 'destructive haunting'.

YE OLDE GATEHOUSE
(Highgate. Map reference: 8)

One of the prominent phantoms in London's ghostlore is Mother Marnes, a rather sinister figure dressed in black who glides along a gallery in Ye Olde Gatehouse. Mother Marnes, along with her cat, was killed for her savings long ago, and perhaps it was her outrage at this which has kept her earthbound. According to a Gatehouse legend, one landlord was so alarmed at seeing her spectre that he had to be rushed to hospital. A curious aspect of this haunting is that it is believed the lady will not appear when there are children or animals in the pub.

THE PLOUGH INN
(Clapham Common. Map reference: 8)

The top storey of this old pub has long had a reputation for being haunted, a number of past landlords having described mysterious manifestations. Some claimed to have seen the resident ghost who was known as Sarah. Thirteen years ago the paranormal activity intensified and it was reported that the staff would only go upstairs in pairs after dark.

One night a barman, who lived on the premises, woke up and saw the apparition which he described as a dark-haired woman clothed in white standing by his open window. He immediately knew that there was something uncanny about her because her hair was not affected by the wind that was filling the curtains. He was even more convinced of it when she melted away. Next day he gave in his notice and left immediately.

The staff described a curious effect the ghost had upon them as being like mild electric shocks, the tingling sensation of which lasted up to a minute.

THE THOMAS À BECKET
(Bermondsey. Map reference: 8)

A gallows used to stand on the site of this pub in the Old Kent Road, which may be the reason for the eerie happenings which have occurred there down the years. Sometimes they were so dramatic that one landlord would not stay by himself on the premises after closing time. This activity was of the type associated with a poltergeist and one of its tricks was to jam bedroom doors so tightly that they had to be broken open.

A typical story of the haunting was the shattering of a beer glass in the hand of a man the moment he declared that he did not believe in the supernatural. Another tradition of the pub was a room in the upper storey which caused customers to lose bets they wagered that they could stay alone in it for half an hour.

I first encountered such stories when I was a reporter years ago and went to the Thomas à Becket to write a feature on sport rather than the paranormal – with a training gym on the first floor it was once famous as the Boxers' Pub.

Merseyside

THE GOLDEN LION
(Rainford. Map reference: 76)

Just before Mrs Nell Cowing gave up the licence of the Golden
Lion in July, 1980, her daughter Nikki talked to a journalist
from the *St Helen's Reporter* about the two ghosts which
haunted the pub. She explained that the previous landlady had
lost her son in the Second World War.

'From the day she got the telegram she locked his bedroom
door and never opened it again,' said Nikki. 'When we moved
in we unlocked the door and all his things were still there intact.
My sister Sally had his bedroom and she has seen him come
walking through the wall where an archway used to be. He was
wearing his uniform.' She added that this military ghost had
also been seen outside on the landing.

The pub's other phantom obviously goes back to the last
century when the premises were used as a girls' boarding
school. Describing this small ghost, Nikki said, 'She looks
about eleven years old and is dressed in the school uniform of
the day with an apron over her dress.'

THE PUNCH BOWL INN
(Sefton. Map reference: 127)

One of the strangest-looking spectres you are likely to
encounter in a pub is at the Punch Bowl Inn where the face and
shoulders only of a young man, surmounted by a halo of mist,
have been seen to float at head-level above the floor. One
legend says that this apparition is of a seafaring man from the
days of the first Queen Elizabeth. As in the case of so many
very old ghosts, any explanation of his background has been
long forgotten.

122

The pub has another nautical phantom but there is nothing odd about his appearance. Sometimes, when seen dressed in seaman's clothing and sitting by a fireplace in one of the ground floor rooms, he has been mistaken for a flesh-and-blood customer – until fading away! It is not surprising to learn that in the past this room was used as a temporary morgue for the bodies of drowned sailors before being interred in the Sefton churchyard.

THE STORK HOTEL
(Billinge. Map reference: 152)

Jack Lyon, said to be Lancashire's last highwayman, was once a frequent visitor to The Stork, and it is a local belief that his dashing phantom sometimes canters through the village on a spectral horse in the direction of the old hostelry. This manifestation is said to occur after midnight has struck and is accompanied by the sound of hooves.

The hotel has its own ghost and this being Lancashire, where the Civil War left an unusual number of phantoms from the Royalist side, one is not surprised to learn that the intruder is a cavalier. Considering his genteel background he is rather a boisterous guest, being inclined to stamp in his riding boots when he moves about the premises. There is also a touch of the poltergeist about him. Members of the staff have reported incidents in which glasses are picked up and hurled to the floor by an invisible hand. But he is not just an unseen force. Quite recently a hotel guest came out of the gentlemen's toilet enquiring where the costume party was being held. He explained that as he was washing his hands a man dressed as a cavalier stood beside him. When a member of the staff went into the toilet to investigate it was deserted.

Perhaps the glass-throwing and stamping is a manifestation of ancient frustration. According to legend the cavalier was not allowed to die valiantly on the battlefield for the royal cause, but as a prisoner of war in the cellars of The Stork which the Parliamentarians used as a place to hold their captives.

Norfolk

THE DUKE'S HEAD HOTEL
(King's Lynn. Map reference: 58)

The Duke's Head Hotel, a large pink and white Renaissance building, overlooks a large square known as Tuesday Market Place. In 1685 it was built on the site of an older inn known as The Gryffyn, which had been standing there since the time of King Henry VIII. The new inn was named after the Duke of York who later became King James II, and in the 18th century it became famous as a coaching inn.

The Duke's Head long had the reputation of being haunted but, unfortunately, the legend has been lost along with the modernisation of the hotel. It would seem that the ghost, whatever it was, took a dislike to the 20th century, preferring the more spacious days when the Duke's Head was a coaching house and not a centre for tourists and their cars.

It is not surprising, however, that a haunting has been connected with the Duke's Head. Some terrible things have taken place in the square under its three tiers of bland Georgian windows. A pillory used to stand beside the inn, while Tuesday Market Place had long been a site of executions.

Wandering about the stalls of the market and enjoying the old-world charm of the buildings ranged about the square, it is hard to imagine that in medieval times unfortunate victims of the witchcraft hysteria were burnt at the stake here and, during periods of religious persecution, heretics also had the faggots heaped about them. Criminals were despatched from a gallows standing in the square.

One of the last executions was on 13 November, 1801, when Peter Donahue, a sergeant of the 30th Foot Regiment, was hanged 'for forgery or for a murder committed on the road leading to Wiggenhall'. The diversity of the sergeant's crimes are intriguing, and perhaps it was his restless spirit that for a while haunted the Duke's Head.

I am inclined to think that the inn was haunted by a ghost going back to the 16th century, the ghost of a servant who was executed in the square for poisoning her mistress.

The horrendous punishment was described in an old book, *The History of the Borough of King's Lynn* by Henry J. Hillen, thus:

'A maidservant was boiled to death on the Tuesday Market Place in 1531. A fire was placed beneath a huge cauldron filled with water and the terrified victim was plunged in as soon as boiling point was reached by means of a chain, thrown over the top of the gibbet. The body was pulled up and down until life was extinct.'

The now-forgotten story of the ghost of the Duke's Head could stem from the execution of a witch, a murderer or the servant girl. If extreme human fear and agony can leave an echo behind it, then it is not surprising such an echo has recurred from time to time in this once-sinister location.

All signs of the horrors which once took place in front of the Duke's Head are long gone except one. If you turn right from the hotel's entrance and walk to the end of the square you will find the old brick Co-operative Insurance building. Above the door there is carved a heart within a diamond-shaped frame. The landlord of the Duke's Head told me that this is a memorial to the death of the maid. According to grim local legend, the impact of the boiling water on the girl's body had the effect of splitting her chest open. Her heart burst from her and struck the wall opposite where the simple carving now marks the spot.

THE OLD FERRY INN
(Horning. Map reference: 110)

The Old Ferry Inn gazes serenely across the River Bure in the heart of the Norfolk Broads as, during the summer season, hundreds of pleasure cruisers pass it daily. Ted Shadbolt, the landlord, told me that there actually was a ferry until a few years ago when 'it was under the water more than on it and we gave it up', thus ending a service which went back to Roman times. The inn itself is a comparatively new building because, on 26 April, 1941, the old building received a direct hit from a German bomb which killed twenty-two people in the bar.

The ghost at the Old Ferry Inn is exclusive in her habits, appearing only at twenty-year intervals. According to the legend, the first building where the inn now stands was a mead house belonging to a monastic order many centuries ago. One summer day several monks sampled so much mead they forgot their vows of chastity.

When a pretty girl walked by on the river bank, the drunken brothers dragged her into the mead house where she was raped. As she struggled they beat her until she went limp. Afterwards, as sanity began to dawn in their sodden minds, they were filled with horror at their crime – and at the pathetic corpse which lay sprawled before them. At nightfall they fearfully pushed it beneath the surface of the Bure to hide the evidence of the outrage.

Since then the shade of the unfortunate girl has made rare appearances at the scene of her death. Mr Shadbolt said he had not personally experienced anything abnormal since he had been at the inn, but an organisation interested in psychic phenomena, the Psychic and Scientific Investigation Group, came to the Old Ferry with their recording instruments. In the room said to be haunted they found sudden and inexplicable drops in temperature during the night.

A description of the ghost had been given by the landlord prior to World War II. He stated that on 25 September, 1936, he was sitting in the inn at about midnight, waiting for the return of a late guest. He dozed off, then suddenly he found himself wide awake.

'I heard a noise, a rustling,' he reported. 'Not three yards from me, in the passage leading to the staircase, was the frail shadowy form of a girl of about twenty-five. She wore a greenish-grey cloak, but it was her face that most attracted my attention. It was beautiful yet deathly white, and had a look of suffering.'

The publican tried to speak to her, but she glided towards the front door and then appeared to vanish through it. The startled man opened the door and saw the wraith disappearing at the river's edge, close to where the ferry was moored.

One of the Inn's guests, taking a stroll before going to bed, corroborated the landlord's story. He said he heard him cry out, and the next moment he was aware of the slight shape of a girl moving past him and into the water.

North Yorkshire

THE ANGEL INN
(Stokesley. Map reference: 6)

Probably one of the most alarming supernatural manifestations in a British pub occurred recently when a disembodied voice swore at a priest who was endeavouring to exorcise it. Norah Atkinson, wife of the licensee of the Angel Inn, told me that the paranormal activity centred on the pub barn which had been converted into a restaurant.

'In the mid-eighteenth century Mass was regularly celebrated in there,' she told me. 'In fact the barn was the first Catholic church in Stokesley. At first mass was said outdoors where our car park is now. The landlord of the day said that the Catholics could use his barn, and twenty-five years later a proper church was built.'

Strangely, considering the religious background of the barn, it has become the haunt of a mischievous entity.

'I often get a feeling of fear,' Mrs Atkinson admitted. 'Things happen which you just cannot answer. Some are daft things like you are standing in the restaurant and all of a sudden the toilets flush simultaneously even though there is no one there. Glasses move by themselves – we've even had them flying at customers.'

Interference with the plumbing and the movement of objects is not at all unusual for pubs with resident poltergeists as this book shows, but in one respect the Angel is unique.

'We used to have candles on the tables in the restaurant,' said Mrs Atkinson. 'But no matter what you did to extinguish them and make sure the doors were locked so that no one could get in during the night, you could guarantee that next morning there would be a candle on one of the tables that would be lit.'

Finally the Atkinsons asked a priest to perform the service of exorcism in the restaurant.

'He explained to us that the burning candle may have had something to do with the candles once used in the Mass,' Mrs Atkinson said. 'But when we took the priest into the place I'll never forget this very deep voice which boomed, "Get out, you bugger, we don't need you here." Clearly there was nobody else there and the priest said it was the ghost. Unfortunately the exorcism did not work and we never got rid of him. Now we just carry on.'

THE SALTERGATE INN
(Saltergate. Map reference: 143)

The inn used to be known as the Wagon and Horses, but the present name is more suitable as it was here the salters came over the moors from Robin Hood's Bay by a secret track to preserve their fish with illegal salt. One is used to hearing of inns which were the headquarters of spirit and tobacco smugglers, but salt smugglers are more of a rarity. They go back to the days of the unpopular salt tax, which was evaded by certain independent individuals who obtained the then precious mineral by boiling cauldrons of seawater over driftwood fires.

In a book on haunted pubs the Saltergate Inn is an exception to the rule – it is definitely not haunted.

'There are no ghosts at the inn,' Ken Matthews, the landlord, said, 'although there are tales of a phantom woman crying on the moors.'

This supernatural wailing is mentioned in a book, *Crying in the Wilderness*, by Brenda H. English, which is set in Saltergate in the 18th century. The wild moors surrounding the inn make an ideal background for such a tale, especially as this is the area of the 'killing pits'. These are sites where once great fires blazed, leaving layers of ash to be seen to this day. It was thought they were the remains of terrible Druid sacrifices.

There is a very intriguing reason why the inn itself is free from supernatural activity.

'The inn was built in 1759,' I was told. 'The first landlord lit a peat fire when he moved in, and from that day to this the fire has not gone out. It was said at the time that if it was not kept continually burning great misfortune could fall upon the inn and its inmates.'

One legend says that the fire keeps an evil spirit imprisoned beneath the hearth. This may be due to the building having been erected on a so-called 'killing pit'. Another version which I heard was that a witch was buried where the inn now stands and the smouldering peat keeps her malignant spirit at bay.

Whatever the reason, the fact remains that the fire still burns as it has done for a couple of centuries.

THE THREE MARINERS
(Scarborough. Map reference: 157)

Today the old waterside tavern known as the Three Mariners no longer serves as an inn but, thanks to the enterprise of Mrs Maggie Mainprize, it has been preserved as a fascinating relic of the past. An inn has stood on this site since 1300, and the building is riddled with secret passages and concealed cupboards. These small, windowless rooms and passages were used by smugglers and by seamen wishing to avoid the press gang. There is a tradition that a tunnel runs from the cellars to the nearby harbour.

One of the inn's showpieces is the Queen Anne Room, complete with antique furniture, and there are secret passages behind its panelling. A small passage runs from a cupboard close to the fireplace to the room next door which is believed to be haunted.

Opposite the Queen Anne Room is the John Paul Jones Room which, according to a strong legend, once sheltered that intrepid American sailor after he had engaged a squadron of English warships off Flamborough Head. During the battle he sank the *Seraphis*, after which his own ship, *Le Bonhomme Richard*, went down. He managed to reach the shore and made his way to Scarborough and the Three Mariners. After hiding here, he fled to France and eventually back to America where he had further encounters with the British navy.

In the days of sail, seamen who were drowned in shipwrecks off Scarborough were carried into the Three Mariners to await burial. One such disaster concerned a Norwegian vessel which foundered with all hands and, as usual, the bodies of the crew washed up were brought to the inn. Soon afterwards the ship's figurehead was found floating, and this too was brought to the inn and erected above the door as a memorial to the unknown sailors. It was a carving of a lady in Grecian-style dress, exposing a pleasant expanse of bosom, and she came to be known as Elvira.

One legend concerning Elvira was that when a bad storm was due she would leave her position on the wall of the Three Mariners and knock at fishermen's doors to warn them of impending disaster. It is an intriguing story but unfortunately Elvira was taken down some time ago and sold to an American who transported her back to his own country.

The haunted room in the Three Mariners has its share of secret recesses, and in one there is a hole in the floor just large enough for a man to squeeze through. From it a rope ladder used to dangle which allowed smugglers to escape to the cellar below, and thence through the secret tunnel to their craft.

The room is reputed to be haunted by the ghost of a headless woman who used to appear as a warning to fishermen not to put to sea. Probably the legend of the animated figurehead stemmed from the activities of this ghost. Why she should be headless, or why she should take an interest in the welfare of fisherfolk is not known today, but stories of her haunting doggedly persist. One concerns a fisherman who, with his cousin, was setting off early for the day's work. As they approached the Three Mariners, he saw the headless spectre in the morning mist.

'The headless lady!' he exclaimed. 'That does it! I'm going home!'

His cousin, who did not see the apparition, laughed at him, perhaps thinking it was an excuse to have a day off. He continued down to the quay, took his boat out and by nightfall had been drowned as the result of a squall.

THE YORK ARMS
(York. Map reference: 171)

York is the most haunted city in Britain apart from London, so it is only to be expected that it has a haunted pub among its array of ghosts. As with many other haunted inns, the phenomena here are caused by a combination of a phantom and a poltergeist force.

'Our ghost is the Grey Lady who also haunts the Theatre Royal – which is a stone's throw from us – and the area round Petergate, Duncan Place and St Leonards Place,' Barry Grayson, the tenant of the York Arms, told me. 'The old legend is that she was a nun who was bricked up for having given birth to a baby, and this was supposed to have happened on the site of the theatre. She has been seen searching for this child.'

He said that he had been warned of the pub's eerie reputation when he arrived and since then certain things had happened 'which have been inexplicable to say the least'.

'My wife went down into the cellar to get some clean towels but before she reached them she was showered with a dozen metal ashtrays which just fell off a shelf,' Mr Grayson said. 'That sent her scurrying upstairs without a doubt.

'Once a pair of bellows came off the wall. They didn't just drop down but were thrown ten feet from the wall. The most extraordinary incident happened when an object fell from a shelf mounted above a door frame – it actually came through the door into the kitchen and struck my wife on the shoulder as she was working. We experimented by knocking it off the shelf two or three dozen times but no way could we emulate what had happened.'

Mr Grayson added that the Grey Lady had been seen on several occasions by the previous licensee and his family.

'He was a no-nonsense ex-policeman but one day he was painting a wall when he looked up and saw her figure in the doorway. He was so startled that he threw his paintbrush at her – and saw it fly right through her. His father-in-law was off work for three months after he saw her!'

Northamptonshire

THE BLACK LION
(Northampton. Map reference: 24)

When a psychical investigation group carried out a vigil in the ancient cellar beneath this pub they were rewarded with the sight of mysterious lights. The lights, seen at the far end of the vault flickering like candles, were only visible for a few moments but during that time two members of the party claimed to see a shadow-like figure moving close to them. Earlier a landlord had seen something like a shape of luminous mist appear in a corner of the cellar where it floated for several minutes before fading away.

Mysterious lights are only a minor part of the phenomena which have occurred at the Black Lion during this century. Unfortunately there is no tradition to explain why the pub should have a supernatural reputation, yet successive licensees have described the inexplicable switching on and off of electric lights, the movement of shadows cast by no living being, and the sound of disembodied footsteps. More dramatic was the experience of one landlord who began telling a man with a dog to get out of his bedroom one night – until he realised that he was addressing a ghost.

SAMUEL PEPYS HOTEL
(Slipton. Map reference: 144)

It is only fitting that Samuel Pepys, who was a guest in such a great number of inns, should have one named after him. And as he enjoyed telling 'stories of spirits', it is also appropriate that the hotel is haunted. News of the haunting came out ten years ago when the landlord and his wife described how, when they were in the bar, they often heard dragging footsteps coming from the room above which they knew to be empty. Around the same time their young nephew stayed at the hotel and told them about an old lady wearing a blue dress who he saw standing over him when he woke up in the night. He said that after a short while she would disappear before his eyes. One thing that all agreed on was that there was nothing frightening about the mysterious visitor.

THE TALBOT HOTEL
(Oundle. Map reference: 156)

The sad spectre which haunts the Talbot Hotel is that of Mary Queen of Scots despite the fact that in her lifetime she never stayed there. With mullioned windows set in its walls of creamy stone and Tudor gables, the inn has been a haven for travellers since before the Norman Conquest – at least since then an inn has always stood on the site of the Talbot which was originally known as The Trabert Inn.

To trace the events which led up to Queen Mary's posthumous connection with the hotel we must go back to 1567 when her despised husband, Darnley, was killed by a gunpowder explosion in a small mansion at Kirk o' Field between ten and eleven on the evening of 9 February.

There was no doubt that the blast was engineered by the Earl of Bothwell who had latterly been a great favourite of the Queen. Rumours swept the country that she had not been unaware of the plot.

A few months after the assassination, Mary wed Bothwell – now universally regarded as the murderer of her husband the King of Scotland (a title he had received through his marriage to her). This new marriage shocked Mary's nobles and estranged the populace.

On 24 July she was taken by the Confederate Lords to Lochleven to sign her abdication in favour of her son who, five days later, was crowned at Stirling.

In May of the following year Mary managed to escape from her island prison and travel south to throw herself on the protection of Queen Elizabeth. The English Queen granted it to her, but she was far from pleased, for the presence in England

134

of this Roman Catholic ex-monarch was a constant source of worry. A large number of English Catholics looked to Mary as the most likely person to restore their faith to the land.

Elizabeth kept Mary under house arrest in various castles but, even so, various plots were hatched for the assassination of the English Queen and the deliverance of Mary. Despite these conspiracies, Elizabeth was reluctant to have Mary brought to trial. It was only when letters were discovered, said to have been written by Mary, approving of the proposed murder of Elizabeth, that she finally consented to Mary being brought before a court.

A commission of Lords sat in judgement on her in September 1586, and sentence of death was pronounced on the 25th of the following month. Even so, it was not until February of the next year that Elizabeth could summon the resolve to sign the death warrant.

On 8 February Mary laid her head on the block at Fotheringay Castle and died with 'the dignity of a queen and the resignation of a martyr'.

At the beginning of the 17th century a man named William Whitwell became the owner of the Talbot. When he heard that James I was going to demolish Fotheringay Castle – the scene of his mother's execution – Whitwell took the opportunity to purchase some of the castle's fittings.

Among these was a large oaken staircase which, prior to the demolition had led to the upper rooms of Fotheringay where Mary Queen of Scots had been a prisoner until her execution. It was down these stairs she walked to keep her appointment with the headsman.

On one of the balustrades there is an impression of a crown which, it was believed, was made by a ring Mary Queen of Scots was wearing when, perhaps overcome with fear, she momentarily clung to the rail.

Local legend has it that the phantom of the Scottish Queen followed the staircase to the Talbot and that Room 5, at the top of the Fotheringay stairs, is a haunted room. Sudden and inexplicable drops in temperature have been reported by visitors staying in the room, while others have described hearing mysterious footsteps. Others have heard a shrill, eerie sound rather like a woman singing, though perhaps 'keening'

135

would be a more apt description.

Once a woman staying in Room 6, next to the haunted room, claimed she heard a woman sobbing bitterly on the other side of the wall. The odd thing was that the room was empty and it was also the anniversary of Mary's execution.

THE WHEATSHEAF
(Daventry. Map reference: 162)

On 7 May, 1641, as King Charles I was celebrating his daughter's wedding to the Prince of Orange, the festivities were interrupted when a Bill was sent to him from the Commons for his signature. It was a Bill of Attainder and its subject was the Catholic nobleman, Viscount Strafford. The King knew that if he put his signature to it, it would mean the execution of a man who had supported him in the past, and to whom he had promised his protection.

Charles was powerless to prevent Strafford's arrest but no noble could be executed without the monarch's signature. At first the King pushed the document away from him, and for two days he refused to sign despite the arguments of bishops and judges and the cries of the mob which had assembled outside Whitehall. But the pressure on the King increased and, finally, the pleas of the Queen to avert trouble by humouring Parliament broke Charles' resistance, and on 9 May he wrote his name at the bottom of the hated paper.

Giving in to Parliament did little to stem the tide of ill-fortune which was flowing against the King. The next year it became clear that only warfare could settle the dispute between the Crown and Commons, and on 22 August, 1642, the King raised the Royal Standard at Nottingham and the Civil War officially began.

In June 1645, Charles found himself with his army at Daventry, in Northamptonshire, where he made The Wheatsheaf Inn his headquarters. Here he began to plan a battle which he hoped would be the turning point of the war. On the night of 13 June the King had dropped off into an uneasy sleep when he suddenly awoke to see a shadowy figure standing in his room. As a trusty guard was posted outside the bedchamber,

Charles was aware that this was no human visitor – it was the spectre of the executed Strafford!

The next morning Charles told his commanders how the viscount had appeared to him. Although he was still grieved over his betrayal, he still felt a loyalty to his King and had returned to the world to warn him against the forthcoming battle. It would end in disaster for the Royalists, the ghost declared.

When the King had finished his gloomy tale, Prince Rupert spoke up, saying that it was probably nothing more than a nightmare. It was not unnatural that the memory of Strafford should weigh heavily on His Majesty's mind and with it doleful thoughts. But, he added, strategy should not be altered because of a bad dream. The plans had been laid carefully and the time had come to thrash the Roundheads. The others agreed, and reluctantly Charles allowed himself to be talked into continuing with the proposed battle. No doubt, as the orders were given and the Royal troops marched to Naseby, twelve miles away, the impression of the visitation faded from the King's mind.

As everyone knows, the King's cause was lost to Cromwell's Ironsides at Naseby. Although Charles behaved with exceptional gallantry throughout the battle, he lost 3,000 men, his 'park of artillery', his baggage and all his personal belongings and papers. Many times afterwards, before and after the Scots handed him over to the English Parliamentarians for the sum of £400,000, Charles was heard to mutter: 'I wish to God I had paid heed to Strafford's warning.'

Today, the interior of The Wheatsheaf has not greatly altered since the six days when Charles was resident there. In the room where he once briefed his officers, a Rotary Club now holds regular meetings. The landlord, Francis Lauwerys, pointed to the panelling which covers the walls of this large chamber.

'That goes back to the Restoration,' he said. 'There was such a feeling for Charles I after his son returned to England that, for a while, this inn became a place of pilgrimage. The reason was that it was at The Wheatsheaf where Charles spent his last few days as a real King. Unfortunately, we can only guess which was the bedroom where he saw the ghost of Strafford.

'Although the front façade does not give any suggestion of age, the place goes back centuries. The oldest part is at the back, and that began as a farmhouse in 1300. In a survey of the local manor made in Tudor times, the actual inn is mentioned as being built in the thirteenth year of Queen Elizabeth's reign, which would put the date at 1571.'

He pointed to a heavy crossbar which could be fitted into sockets across one of the old doors. 'This was to protect the serving wenches in the old days,' he explained. 'Once the gallants had taken their fill of wine it took more than ordinary locks to save the girls from them. And look, the door handles have been forged by a blacksmith.'

One of the wings is completely shut up, and there are rooms in the building which have not been opened for a century.

'Although it is a long time since Charles saw the ghost here, there is still something uncanny about the place,' Mr Lauwerys said. 'One cannot help feeling a great sense of the past, but I think it is more than that. People here are conscious of a strange atmosphere, and it builds up each year towards midsummer. In fact, the critical period is the sixth of June – the anniversary of the King's arrival.

'I believe the place is haunted still by something going back to that time, perhaps in the way that people on earth can see the light from a star when that star may no longer be in existence. And I think there are certain people who get these sensations from the past although they cannot explain why. Many people do here, anyway, and so do dogs. Sometimes they act very concerned, as though they can see something that we can't. There is more to this inn than just a legend, the whole feeling about the place is strange.'

Northumberland

THE CROSS INN
(Alnwick. Map reference: 44)

On 2 January, 1979, *The Sunday Post* reported that vandals had smashed the window of the Cross Inn which is known locally as 'The Dirty Bottles'. Unfortunately there is nothing rare about stories of vandalism, but the reason that this one was featured in the paper was because of a curse which was traditionally supposed to be connected with the inn's window display.

The legend goes that two centuries ago the person who arranged a number of bottles in the window collapsed and died the moment the job was completed. The belief grew that the same fate would befall anyone else who moved the bottles. This could be regarded as a quaint example of pub folklore, yet it was still potent enough for the window to be replaced hurriedly without the remaining bottles being touched – even the broken pieces of bottle glass which resulted from the act of vandalism were left undisturbed.

THE LORD CREWE ARMS
(Blanchland. Map reference: 102)

If you follow the old Hexham Road down from the fells of Hexhamshire Common, when the glow of the dying sun is diffused through a line of distant trees and dusk is gathering in the Derwent Valley, it is not hard to imagine the ghostly presence of Dorothy Forster gliding behind you. The only sound is the murmur of the nearby beck, the cough of a grouse and the melancholy call of the curlew. The road, often little more than a track, runs gently down between crumbling dry stone walls and takes you past Penny Pie Farm and several grey ruins marking long abandoned lead mines. And then, without warning, the mellow stone roofs of Blanchland are magically before you.

Originally a Premonstratensian abbey, the village retains its former monastic layout with buildings of millstone grit surrounding a large square. At the north end is a battlemented gate tower, the ancient abbey church and the Lord Crewe Arms which was once the abbot's guest house.

One of the best preserved country villages in Britain, Blanchland has been protected through the centuries by its isolation. Situated in a narrow part of the Derwent Valley, it is so well screened by fell and forest that you are only aware of it once you have reached it. Even today the nearest railway station is ten miles away. Being close to the border, this secrecy of position was important to the abbey when Scots' raiding parties made forays into England.

It is recorded that in 1327 a large party of these raiders set out to loot Blanchland. In those days only a drovers' track connected it with the outside world and when a thick mist fell the Scots lost their way. Seeing the shielding mist as divine intervention, the White Monks tolled a *Te Deum* of thanksgiving, but the sonorous voices of the bells echoing along the valley led the marauders to the abbey. The monks were put to the sword and their bodies are said to lie beneath a stone cross which stands ancient and proud in the churchyard.

It used to be a local belief that on each anniversary of the massacre the church bells tolled mysteriously at midnight and the dim figures of the murdered monks might be seen in the church precincts, next to the Lord Crewe Arms. The spectre of the slain abbot was said to walk through the village to the bridge which crosses the River Derwent into Durham. But it is not his ghost which concerns us but that of Dorothy Forster who, in 1715, was involved in the first Jacobite Rebellion when her brother Tom led forces loyal to the Old Pretender against George I. The enthusiastic but disorganised uprising ended disastrously and Tom Forster would have been hanged, drawn and quartered had it not been for an escape organised by his sister.

Today her portrait hangs in the haunted tower of the Lord Crewe Arms and, looking at her mild features, it is hard to imagine the determination which took her to London in disguise to free her brother from Newgate Prison.

Dorothy was born in the latter part of the 17th century, the youngest of a family of six. Their mother died while they were young and their father Sir Thomas Forster married again. Soon afterwards his wife was killed in a shooting accident and he married for a third time. Dorothy and her brother Tom did not find it easy to accept their stepmother and were inclined to seek refuge in a world of their own making. As Dorothy grew she was said to resemble in beauty her mother's sister, also named Dorothy, who, at the age of twenty-six, had married the Bishop of Durham who was forty years her senior. (Despite the age difference, the marriage was noted for its happiness.) Her married name was Crewe, which explains how the hotel at Blanchland gets the name of the Lord Crewe Arms.

When Dorothy's Uncle Ferdinado was killed in a duel Tom became heir to the Forsters' Bamburgh estate. Aunt Dorothy Crewe watched over the two children with great affection, and it was due to her that Tom later went to study at St John's College, Cambridge. Here he began to show the symptoms which were to characterise his life, and which were in such contrast to his sister. At college he preferred pleasure to study and after four terms he returned to Bamburgh Manor a scholastic failure. With him came an agreeable young man named Anthony Hilyard who had been his tutor.

For the next two years Tom and Dorothy lived under the supervision of Aunt Dorothy. It was a happy time for them. Tom passed the days in the agreeable companionship of his sister, the evenings in drinking and gaming with local blades like himself. Dorothy was delighted to have her brother with her, there were frequent parties and she was receiving tuition from Mr Hilyard who was pleasantly in love with her.

The idyll was interrupted in 1709 when Tom was faced with bankruptcy, his fortune having been squandered on cards, wine and horses. Aunt Dorothy's husband, the Bishop of Durham, saved the situation by buying Tom's estates and settling his debts. Tom and Dorothy were left with an income of £500 a year, and were allowed to go on living at the Bamburgh manor.

Meanwhile Tom's father had retired from Parliament and Tom had taken his seat as the Tory member for Northumberland. It was probably at this time that the Jacobite cause began

141

to interest him. No doubt this was encouraged by his friendship with young Lord Derwentwater, who had grown up in the French court of the Old Pretender, James III. In 1710 Derwentwater returned to Dilston Hall, his ancestral home, which was situated close to Blanchland. In the same year Tom and Dorothy went to live at the village in the old abbot's guest house, now the Lord Crewe Arms, at their aunt's request. She believed Tom would be further from temptation there. As they travelled from Hexham to Blanchland they met Lord Derwentwater. His youth and charm, and manners acquired in France, caused Dorothy to describe him as 'the most complete gentleman I have ever seen'.

Although at Blanchland Tom may have missed his Bamburgh companions, he was happy to be close to Dilston Hall and the company of his elegant friend. It seemed the idyll which he and his sister enjoyed at Bamburgh had returned. Life at Blanchland centred around hunting parties made up of young local people, and social gatherings at Dilston Hall and the converted abbey which was now the home of Tom and Dorothy.

During this period, legend says, Dorothy fell in love with Lord Derwentwater. It was to be expected that a young and intelligent girl should be attracted to such an accomplished and gentle man. The lovers left messages for each other hidden at the foot of a huge holly tree on the road between Blanchland and Dilston Hall. According to the Reverend Paulin, the Vicar of Blanchland, a road widening scheme was recently dropped because it would have meant the destruction of this giant holly.

Unfortunately they were divided on the question of religion. Dorothy Forster was a staunch Protestant. When her faith wavered for the sake of the man she loved, her uncle the Bishop emphatically reminded her of her duty to the Church of England. She asked Lord Derwentwater if it would be possible for him to change from the Church of Rome and he replied, 'Not until the Pope is converted.'

No doubt the young couple were able to put the question to the back of their minds when they met at parties or went for rides over the fells, but sooner or later they knew that the problem would have to be faced. At length they both realised that as long as they held to their beliefs there could be no question of a future for them and they agreed to part.

Dorothy went back to Bamburgh and in 1712 Lord Derwentwater married a woman of his own faith named Anna Webb.

Time passed sadly for Dorothy while her brother became more and more involved in Jacobite politics. In 1714 Queen Anne died and George I was imported from Hanover. Realising that troubled times lay ahead, Aunt Dorothy Crewe sent a warning to her nephew, urging him to burn all papers which might connect him with Jacobites.

The advice came too late. On 10 January 1715, Tom was expelled from Parliament. Later a warrant was issued for his arrest and he and his sister travelled to Blanchland whose isolation they believed would give them some measure of safety. Meanwhile the Jacobite Rebellion broke out in East Scotland under the Earl of Mar, and on 9 September the Pretender was proclaimed in the small market town of Kirk-Michael.

Lord Derwentwater told Tom and Dorothy that he was going to support the rebels, declaring his mistaken belief that throughout Britain the people were eager for the chance to throw off the yoke of the German king who could not even speak his subjects' language. He also believed English soldiers would not fight against Englishmen, and the Hanoverian's only defence would be his foreign mercenaries. Tom had equal enthusiasm for the revolt, and there was talk of his taking command of the Northumberland rebels who were ready to rise in sympathy with the Scots.

Doubtless Tom Forster and Lord Derwentwater felt they were taking part in history when they rode off to Warkworth, to the accompaniment of trumpet fanfares from the ruins of the local castle, to read the Proclamation of Rebellion to a following of sixty men. A few days later at Brampton in Cumbria Tom was made the official commander of the rebels and became known as 'The Pretender's General'. But his glory was short-lived. On 14 November the Jacobite army surrendered at Preston and fifteen hundred prisoners were taken by the royal army. Among those taken to London to stand trial were Tom Forster and Lord Derwentwater.

News of the disaster reached Dorothy when Anthony

Hilyard, who had followed Tom through the rebellion, returned to Blanchland. She told him that they must set out for London immediately, explaining that she had a cousin Mary there who was married to Lord Cowper, the Lord Chancellor, and she might be able to intercede with him on Tom's behalf. She persuaded her tutor to dress as a blacksmith. She would pose as his sister and ride behind him, the disguise being necessary as the sport of hunting down Jacobites had begun.

One can only feel admiration for Dorothy who day after day rode over rough tracks with snow often up to the horse's knees. On 9 December they arrived in London where they lodged near Drury Lane with a blacksmith from Bamburgh who was an old friend.

Dorothy went to see her cousin, Lady Cowper. She was sympathetic but her most practical assistance was only to get permission for Dorothy to visit Tom in Newgate. From then on she saw him every day, and when it was time to leave she made a point of liberally tipping the warder. Tom, as befitted a gentleman with money, had been given good quarters with his own drawing room.

It was a miserable time for Dorothy. As yet she did not know when Tom would stand trial and she received a note from Lord Derwentwater in the Tower of London asking her to visit him. She was able to see him once and bid him farewell before he was beheaded.

Four days before his execution Lord Derwentwater was asked to acknowledge George I and the Protestant religion. He refused and in doing so lost the chance of a pardon. He met his end on 24 February 1716, with a calmness which awed the spectators into silence. Later his wife gave Dorothy one of his rings.

The death of Lord Derwentwater left no doubt in Dorothy's mind as to Tom's chances. Indeed, as he did not qualify to be a Tower prisoner, he could not expect the swift stroke of the headsman's axe but the barbaric death of official mutilation.

Hilyard was amazed at the way Dorothy, brought up so peacefully in the North, set about arranging her brother's escape. On her next visit to Newgate she broke down in tears before the friendly warder as he was escorting her from Tom's rooms.

'I wish there was something I could do to help, my lady,' he said. It was the psychological moment to mention an escape. Within minutes the conversation reached a solid financial basis. The warder agreed to help for five hundred guineas.

The first thing he would do was take a wax impression of the master key. Dorothy's blacksmith landlord could easily make a key from this. Hilyard, meanwhile, searched Thameside taverns until he found a sea captain who was willing to take an un-named gentleman to France from the Essex coast for the consideration of fifty guineas.

On 7 April, 1716, a Bill of Indictment was laid against Tom Forster and his trial was arranged for 14 April. The time had come. During a visit Dorothy slipped him the duplicate key, then she left and waited at the Salutation Tavern in Newgate Street where Hilyard had stabled four thoroughbred horses.

On the evening of the 10th, Tom invited Pitts, the Prison Governor, to have supper with him. He had done this before and the Governor enjoyed his conversation, and after the meal was cleared away the wine began to flow.

As midnight approached, Tom asked his valet to fetch more wine. The man went off with the head-keeper's servant who was responsible for the wine cellar key. As the prison servant entered the vault, the door was slammed and the key turned in the lock. In his drawing room Tom rose, smiled at the Governor and said, 'Pray, excuse me a moment.' The Governor smiled back, making a little joke about the amount of wine he had consumed. Tom walked out into the corridor where his man was waiting.

A few minutes later Pitts, alarm suddenly piercing his alcoholic euphoria, went to the door to find it had been locked by the duplicate master key which had also unlocked an outside door of the prison. In the street Dorothy and Hilyard were waiting for the two fugitives with the horses and soon they were galloping through the night to Rochford where the ship was ready to sail.

Dorothy and Hilyard quietly settled their affairs in London and then rode north in the early spring sunshine. It was a happier journey than the last, yet Dorothy was sad with the thought that her brother was an exile in Rome and that she would probably never see him again. No doubt her memory focussed on her life in Blanchland when everything had been happy, when Tom had not been the 'Pretender's General' but a jolly young squire and she had ridden out along the Old Hexham Road to meet the charming Lord Derwentwater. Everything had changed so suddenly. All that remained of the dear past was the faithful Hilyard riding at her side. Legend says he asked her to marry him, but to her he was always a companion and she could not imagine him as anything closer. Gently she rejected him. Later Lord Crewe made him a canon at Durham Cathedral while Dorothy returned to live at Bamburgh.

On 3 November 1738, Tom Forster died at Boulogne, as close to England as he could safely be. As time went by and Dorothy's adventure receded into the past, she took up the threads of ordinary life again. An inscription on the frame of her portrait hanging in the tower of the Lord Crewe Arms says she married John Armstrong of Berryhill and died in 1767.

And so the story of the escape of the Pretender's General came to its end, remembered by a few paragraphs in old history books, by local legend – and the ghost of Dorothy Forster.

Roger West was the proprietor of the Lord Crewe Arms when I visited Blanchland, and he told me, 'I must admit I was sceptical when I came here, but I have talked to several people who have seen her and now I would not be surprised at all if I saw her. In the haunted wing she manifests herself by a series of knocks, and by gently shaking the bed of the occupant of the room. It seems this only affects ladies . . . it is as though there is something she wants to communicate to them.

'A famous medium came up from London and went into a trance in Dorothy Forster's sitting room. She did not know Blanchland, but it was amazing the things she told us about its history. Some of them we did not know ourselves, but when we checked up we found she was right. She said the tower is very psychically charged but it is not harmful.'

The vicar, the Reverend Paulin, said that the phantom is quite accepted by many villagers. 'I suppose souls do feel a particular affection for places where they have been happy,' he added. Local people agree that Lady Dorothy is most likely to be seen around the end of September.

While staying at the Lord Crewe Arms, a young woman told

me of her experience in the haunted room, though at that time she had no idea that it was haunted. Tired by a long drive from London she went to sleep straight away after supper.

'In the night I suddenly found myself wide awake,' she said. 'I had the feeling that someone – or something – had banged into the end of the bed. At first I thought a person was actually moving in the room. I must admit I was very startled, and this gave me a sensation of fright. There was a sort of knocking, and it sounded as though the door of the cupboard was opened.

'The room was pitch black, and I lay for some time trying to summon up the courage to switch on the light. Perhaps I was afraid of what I might see if I did. But as soon as I did – the room was empty of course – the feeling of fear diminished and the awareness of a strange unseen "presence" in the room gradually left me.

'It was not until the next morning I was told that this is the way the ghost manifests herself. Looking on the experience in retrospect I felt I had been foolish to have been frightened – I realised I had been left with only a deep impression of sadness.'

THE WELLINGTON HOTEL
(Riding Mill. Map reference: 160)

The Wellington Hotel is reputed to be haunted by the victim of a witches' coven, and with the story comes the echo of the most fantastic witch trial to be held in the North. It was a private house when it was a meeting place for witches, having been built in 1660 by Thomas Errington, a local gentleman and postmaster.

Landlord Peter Scott explained that the house became an inn when the main Newcastle-Hexham Road was diverted through Riding Mill in 1822. Recent renovations in the building revealed an old kitchen which had been closed up and is now an extension to the bar. It is known as The Little Back Room, and it is here that the ghost of Anne Armstrong returns to the scene of her murder.

Anne's belief that she was in the clutches of evil forces began simply enough when she had an argument with an old woman over some eggs. Anne won the petty tiff, but later she became

147

convinced the market woman had given her the evil eye.

This sensation of being cursed was followed by Anne going into hysterical trances. When revived from them, she would recount extraordinary stories of witches and their sabbats. One can still read her accounts and accusations because, on 5 February 1672, she made depositions to Newcastle magistrates, charging several women with the crime of witchcraft.

In her statement she particularly indicted one Ann Forster who, she declared, 'came with a bridle and bridled her, changed her into a horse and rode upon her till they came to the rest of her companions at Riding Mill Bridge End, where they usually met'. The women then enjoyed themselves with revels and singing and dancing.

'At the same time,' stated Anne, 'they were constantly changing shape.' This continued until they finally rode the bewitched girl home again.

In her deposition, Anne added that a rope hung from the ceiling of what is now The Little Back Room at the Wellington, and that this provided food for the witches' feasts. She explained, 'By swinging on a rope tied to the rafter whereupon all manner of things were set upon the table – broth, chickens, cheese, mutton and bottles of sac.' She said that, at the 'Rideing House', as the Wellington was originally named, the witches rode about the room on dishes and egg-shells, changing their forms at will into cats, greyhounds, hares and bees.

This evidence was used in the Northumbrian witch trial of 1673. Elaborating on her statement before the judge, Anne Armstrong added that the witches 'danced with their devils', and one of them, by name of Anne Baites, went so far as to describe her own particular demon as her 'Protector and Blessed Saviour', which was rather odd because he was in the habit of beating her brutally when she was slow attending to his wants.

In describing the unholy meeting to the court, these words of Anne Armstrong are still to be found on an old document:

> . . . their protector (the Devil) which they called their god, sitting, at the head of the table in a gold chaire, as she thought; and a rope hanging over the roome which everyone touched three several times and whatever was desired was sett upon the table . . . of several kindes of

meat and drink and when they had eaten, she that was last drew the table and kept the reversions. Ann Forster did swing upon the rope and upon the first swing she gott a cheese and upon the second she gott a beatment of wheatflower and upon the third swing she gott about half a quarter of butter, to kneed the flour withall, they having noe power to gett water.

Unfortunately, the records of the trial of the five women accused by Anne are incomplete and we do not know the fate of Ann Forster and Anne Baites and their companions. If the old legend concerning the haunting of the Wellington is to be believed, some of the women, if not all, must have been released. Perhaps Anne's stories were too far-fetched even for those credulous days.

In revenge for the accusations, the witches of Riding Mill managed to lure Anne Armstrong into the very room where they held their sabbats. Here they hanged her with the same rope she claimed was used to obtain the magical provisions. Little wonder the room was sealed up with such a dreadful tale attached to it, especially as for nearly three centuries villagers there have believed that Anne Armstrong has periodically revisited the scene of her execution.

Nottinghamshire

THE TRIP TO JERUSALEM
(Nottingham. Map reference: 158)

One of England's most famous pubs stands at the base of a cliff upon which looms the vast bulk of Nottingham Castle. It is white with tall chimneys and a roof of red tiles and the back seems to disappear into the cliff-face. This is not surprising when the visitor realises that most of its rooms are excavated from the living rock, and it is connected to the warren of tunnels which honeycomb the cliff beneath the castle. High on the wall is a sign which proclaims, *Ye Olde Trip to Jerusalem 1189 AD*, while beneath it another declares it to be the oldest inn in England.

The curious name comes from the time, in the reign of King Richard I, when crusaders were travelling from all over England to fight for the Cross in Palestine. On their way to embark for the Holy Land it was customary for many to stay at the inn for refreshment. The word 'trypp' is the old English word for 'halt'.

The inn itself is as curious as its name. It has chimneys which emerge from the natural rock above it, and ceilings where roots writhe out of crevices to mingle with old spider webs. There is a smell of deep earth in these excavated chambers. In the cellar there is a tiny aperture said to be the mouth of a speaking tube once chiselled out to connect the inn to the fortress perched above.

A brochure given away at the bar states:

> The inn forms a splendid example of the rock habitations once plentiful in Nottingham. The majority of the rooms are literally caverns scooped in the rock itself and spacious cellars and brewhouses are of the same primitive architecture. The visitor to the interior, though he be but slightly acquainted with the stirring events which have

been enacted in and about the famous castle of Nottingham, will go away with the impression that he has indeed trodden upon ground of historical importance.

The text adds that if the visitor passes from the cellars up a flight of narrow steps, he will have access to a small rock-hewn chamber from which another stairway (now sealed by bricks) led to the fortifications overhead. In this room there are ancient weapons, curios connected with the inn and skulls and other objects dug up in the vicinity.

Before the Trip to Jerusalem became a public inn nearly eight centuries ago, it was the brewhouse for the castle. As the castle is linked with the haunting of the inn, it is worth noting that it was first built by William the Conqueror in 1068.

Like the castle and the inn itself, the haunting of The Trip to Jerusalem has its roots deep in history. There have been many reports of ghostly sounds which were heard to echo through the walls of the inn's subterranean chambers. They were not random sounds but regular, as though someone or something were pacing up and down, and they were believed to emanate from what was once a dungeon known as 'Mortimer's Hole'.

A strange happening occurred during World War II when some American servicemen walked out of the inn late at night. It seems they heard the voice of a woman above their heads, screaming words in a foreign language. People familiar with local legend decided that what the G.I.s heard the disembodied voice cry was *'Bel fitz, eiez pitie du gentil Mortimer!'*

To try and find an explanation for this phantom phrase, we must go back to the reign of King Edward III. When Edward II was overthrown by his Queen, Isabella, and her lover Roger Mortimer, Parliament offered the Crown of England to his eldest son, Prince Edward. The boy, who was barely fifteen at the time, refused to accept it until his father had officially abdicated.

When the captive monarch tearfully renounced his throne, Edward III was crowned on 24 January 1327, but the ceremony made him sovereign in name only. The real power remained in the hands of his mother, Queen Isabella, and her paramour Mortimer, who had been created Earl of March.

To begin with, the deposed Edward II was treated reasonably as a prisoner but since Isabella had learned to love

Mortimer she also learned to hate her husband. Soon it was obvious she was revenging herself for the neglect he had shown her in the past.

In the spring he was imprisoned successively in the castles of Corfe, Bristol and Berkeley.

On the night of 21 September 1327, shrieks were heard from within the walls of Berkeley Castle. The King had been horribly murdered by means of a red-hot spit. There can be little doubt that the murder was committed on the command of Mortimer.

When he was seventeen Edward III became determined to stop being a puppet ruler, and to avenge his father.

At the time Isabella and Mortimer were staying in Nottingham Castle, well guarded by picked Welsh troops. It would have been impossible to have taken the castle by direct attack, but the loyal castellan revealed to the King an underground tunnel which led through the rock into the precincts of the fortress.

At midnight, on 19 October 1330, twenty-four of the King's chosen companions came to the Trip to Jerusalem, crept through the secret tunnel and found Edward waiting outside his mother's door. They burst in and the King himself seized Mortimer, ignoring Isabella's plea, '*Bel fitz, eiez pitie du gentil Mortimer!*' – 'Fair son, have pity on the gentle Mortimer!'.

According to tradition, Mortimer was placed in a dungeon carved in the rock beneath the castle which is still known as Mortimer's Hole. Here he must have constantly paced up and down, dreading the fate he knew was in store for him.

He was later taken to London where he was accused of having usurped the King's authority and having 'murdered and killed the King's father'. Tactfully, no mention was made of his liaison with Queen Isabella. On 29 November he was drawn on a hide from the Tower of London to Tyburn where he was the first prisoner to be hanged. His royal mistress was imprisoned for the remaining twenty-eight years of her life in Castle Rising in Norfolk.

Oxfordshire

THE BEAR
(Woodstock. Map reference: 10)

Currents of history have washed round the 12th century Bear at Woodstock as the tide washes round a rock. The earliest records of the royal manor at Woodstock go back fifty years before the Norman invasion of England, when King Ethelred held a council meeting there, no doubt to grumble about the Vikings who were demanding such huge sums of silver to leave his realm in peace. Later, it was used as a base for successive kings who enjoyed hunting the red deer and wild boar in the surrounding forests.

During the centuries, while history was being made at Woodstock, The Bear – now the Bear Hotel – has continued to offer hospitality to travellers and ale to its regulars who doubtless discussed the mysterious happenings at the inn from time to time. It has a haunted room where footsteps have been heard to echo at the dead of night, and where guests' belongings are disarrayed by invisible hands. A film star who was staying at the inn during the production of a film in 1967 declared that she was woken up by the sound of phantom feet; later a member of the production team moved out of the room after only one night.

At the time, the landlord, Mr Fulford-Talbot, was reported as saying that he knew of four other cases of guests having similar experiences in the same room.

THE BIRD CAGE
(Thame. Map reference: 16)

Thame is justly famous for its old buildings, and of these there can be no doubt that the gabled and timber-framed Bird Cage

Inn is the most fascinating. It is regarded as the oldest in Thame, for there are records of its being there in 1430, although it is quite possible that it is older than that. Its unusual name may have come from the 'cage' which was one of the market structures in which offenders were locked before being subjected to the nearby whipping post or the stocks.

'The first clue I had that the place was haunted was from an old boy who comes in here, by name of Jack Fudge,' Mrs Pat Neville, wife of the landlord, told me. 'He used to mix all his drinks in one pot and then he'd sort of mumble: "Have you seen the ghost yet? Have you heard the knocking?" But then I only used to laugh at him.

'Then, when we had been here about three months, I used to wake up in the night and feel vaguely frightened. Then I was sure there was something uncanny here when we had two cameramen as guests. They were working on a film called *Buttercup Chain*, and they shared a double room. After the first night one came down and said, "You've got a ghost up there." I thought he was kidding, especially when his friend said, "Don't be so stupid. I slept in the same room and saw nothing." But next morning he nearly fell down the stairs, all bug-eyed he was, and he said, "There *is* a bloody ghost up there!" '

Mrs Neville might have got an inkling of the truth when an archaeologist arrived and asked if he could inspect the Bird Cage. He was particularly interested in the upper storey which stands like a squat tower at one end of the building.

'He formed the opinion that once lepers had been isolated up there,' she said. 'He found a trapdoor which he thought had been used when monks or nuns, the only people who fed lepers, passed up food in baskets on the end of long poles.

'One night I thought I'd find out about this haunting. I went up to the bedroom of my son, Nicky, and sat on a chair. I dozed off, but suddenly I was awake with a sensation of sheer terror and I leapt out of the chair thinking, "I must get downstairs!"

'There were a lot of metal coathangers on a rail in the corner of the room and as I went to the door they clattered, just as if someone had flicked them. I thought for a moment the window must have been open and they had been moved by a breeze, but as I went through the door I hastily glanced at the window and saw it was shut tight. I felt so frightened I flew down the stairs as though the hounds of hell were after me.'

Mrs Neville said that after that the knocking started.

'If only you had heard that knocking!' she exclaimed. 'It went on for an hour at least.'

It started in the early hours of the morning, but always stopped at 4 am when she heard the town clock striking.

A psychical research group began to investigate the phenomenon, holding sessions in the upper part of the Bird Cage every Saturday night. They told Mrs Neville that at 4 o'clock one morning the ghost communicated the words 'Go away! Go away! I do not want to hear anything more from you!' It seemed to be panicking.

Soon afterwards other manifestations took place.

On one occasion, after Radio Oxford had done a programme on the Bird Cage, a customer was leaning against the bar making a mockery of the whole thing and saying he did not believe in ghosts. Mrs Neville replied, 'If you don't believe, that's OK, but let's not talk about it. I believe now, although I didn't used to . . .' and, as she said this, a mug which was hanging on a hook rose up and struck her painfully on the back of the neck.

'At first I thought the nail had come out,' she explained. 'I was just going to put the mug to one side when the customer went deathly pale and ran from the bar. Another customer had seen the whole thing and said the mug lifted from the hook as though carried by an invisible hand.'

What was more serious was that Mrs Neville's children began to be affected. Her daughter, Debbie, had to move downstairs because she was so frightened, saying that at night she 'felt' the ghost. On another occasion, her son Chris told her that he had had a dreadful night. 'That ghost was whispering to me,' he said.

It was then Mrs Neville climbed to the high haunted part of the Bird Cage to have a confrontation with the entity.

'I felt a real Charlie speaking out loud in an empty room,' she recalled, 'but I felt I had to do it. I said, "You are beginning to frighten my children. I don't mind you being here, as long as you don't hurt anybody . . ."' For a while she continued to speak to the unseen spirit in this vein.

'Strangely enough the knocking stopped,' she said. 'We did not hear it again, although I know the ghost is still around.'

After my visit to the Bird Cage I contacted Edna Weston of Watford who, with her husband Ron, was a member of the psychical research group which regularly visited the Bird Cage.

'The visit to the Bird Cage was my first contact with psychical phenomena,' she said, 'and I was terrified. We went up to the room in the top of the inn and sat concentrating until there was suddenly a furious knocking.'

She said it was terribly loud, and the leader of the group questioned the spirit in the usual way of one knock for 'yes', two knocks for 'no' and so on.

Gradually, through this laborious communication channel, they learnt that the spirit was that of a leper who had been kept in the room at the top of the building. He had met his death when the townsfolk of Thame stoned him, not wanting to have anyone afflicted with such a horrible disease in their midst.

'He was very bitter and unhappy,' said Mrs Weston, 'and when we suggested praying to alleviate his earthbound condition he went wild. Through his knocking he told us he did not believe in God, that he hated people, that he did not want us to disturb him, and finally said "Go, or I will kill you!" After that there was nothing more we could do for our presence seemed only to aggravate the tragic ghost.'

THE CROWN
(Pishill. Map reference: 47)

An inn which must have one of the largest priest-holes on record is The Crown which stands by Christmas Common at Pishill. The hiding place under the roof was recently opened to reveal enough space for the accommodation of thirty priests. And it was from this sanctuary that Father Dominique rushed to give his life for the woman he loved.

When Patrick King took over the inn he traced its history back to the 11th century when it was a small tavern attached to a farm. It was rebuilt on a larger scale in the 15th century.

'The area round here has always been a Catholic strong-hold,' Mr King explained. 'Therefore it was natural when the Reformation came that steps should be taken to protect priests.

Hence the large priest-hole which was constructed under the roof. The haunting of the place dates back to those times.'

In order not to arouse the suspicions of the authorities (and to account for the surprising amount of food consumed on the premises), the ordinary business of the inn had to continue when the fugitive priests were sheltering there. While a priest called Father Dominique was hiding upstairs, a young woman named Elizabeth came to stay at the inn. One night when Dominique came down to exercise they met, and soon a bond of affection grew between them.

Night after night they held their trysts, and in a romantic mood Elizabeth buried a golden coin near the barn as a token of her love. The perils of their situation only served to intensify their feelings. Elizabeth did not ponder too deeply on the fact that she had fallen in love with a priest bound by an oath of chastity – and a priest on the run, at that!

One day a young nobleman paused at the inn for a meal. He drank too much and, catching sight of Elizabeth, tried to make a conquest. When she rebuffed his attentions, wounded pride turned his lavish compliments to loud obscenities which floated up to where Dominique lay under the rafters.

Thinking of nothing but the insults which were being heaped upon Elizabeth, the priest left his hiding place, leapt down the stairs and, seizing a sword from the wall, fought a duel with the young man. Priests have little knowledge of swordplay, and within a few moments Father Dominique sank to the ground mortally wounded. His body was later buried in the Pishill churchyard.

Over the years since the fatal encounter many people have declared they have seen the ghost of the gallant priest.

'They describe him as a man in a black cloak with a big hat,' said Mr King. 'I have not seen him myself, but I do not disbelieve the stories about his appearances because there is another manifestation connected with him which I am often aware of. In fact, we are conscious of it all the time. It is a thumping sound which comes from near the roof. When I first came here and heard it, I would drop whatever I was doing and search every room upstairs, but I soon gave that up. There is never anyone up there that I can see when I hear that thump! thump!

'Spiritualists have held seances here and achieved some remarkable results. A message came through recently warning that the end of the inn would come by fire.'

The spirit communication did not indicate when this catastrophe would take place, but I hope it is not during my lifetime, for The Crown is one of those inns that you wish to visit again and again.

THE GEORGE
(Dorchester. Map reference: 68)

This picturesque old coaching inn is haunted by the phantom of a young woman who has been described as tragic and sad-looking. Today no legend exists which might give a clue to the unhappiness which she must have suffered when she was alive. All that is known is that her white figure has been seen in quite recent times in what is known as the Vicar's Room. Here she is said to look sadly at the four-poster bed before turning round and fading away. Did she, or someone close to her, die in that room, or does her interest in the bed have a more worldly connotation? Surely not in the Vicar's Room!

THE GEORGE
(Wallingford. Map reference: 70)

The scene of the haunting at The George is the aptly named Tear-Drop Room, so called because the wall opposite its small-paned window is decorated with a shower of painted droplets. These are pear-shaped and pear-sized and there is a slight crudeness about their execution as though they have been drawn by a talented child or a primitive artist. The painting is obviously very old, no doubt dating from the time when, in a world without wall paper, decorations were painted straight on to the plaster.

A local school teacher, Peter Davis, was so fascinated by The George's history that he made it the subject for a thesis when he was a student at training college.

'There seems to be no doubt that the Tear-Drop Room is

haunted,' he said. 'It is the ghost of a landlord's daughter who saw her lover murdered. The shock was so great that she went insane and had to be locked up in a room at the inn – the Tear-Drop Room.'

Apparently the poor girl never stopped crying. She mixed soot from the chimney with her tears and drew the tear-drop design on the wall. The legend gives no indication as to why the girl's lover was killed, but Peter Davis believes the murdered man might have been a certain Sergeant John Hobson. Records show that he was killed in a room of the tavern on 3 March 1626.

In the days prior to the Civil War, Wallingford was full of soldiers who were so unruly that on 9 February, 1626, a gallows was erected in the market place in order to force martial law upon the troops. A contemporary entry in the Wallingford Minute Book commented: '. . . the gibbet bred a good deal of peace amongst us, thanks be to God.'

'It is possible the landlord's daughter was in love with John Hobson and saw him killed in a brawl at the inn,' Mr Davis explained, 'after which she traced the tear-drops with her finger. Although the effect is marvellous, it is hardly the work of a trained artist.'

To Peter Davis' knowledge, the last time the ghost of the unhappy girl was seen was in 1968.

'I was doing some research at The George for my thesis when I met a lady who had spent the night there as a guest,' he said. 'She seemed rather upset and told me that, during the night, she had woken up to see a young woman standing by her bed.

'At first she thought it was a maid, and asked what she was doing there in the dead of night. It was then she noticed the figure seemed very sorrowful – there appeared to be tears flowing down her cheeks. The lady felt a wave of deep sadness pass over her as though the sorrow of the ghost was communicating itself to her. Then the figure slowly turned and went straight through the Tear-Drop Wall!

'I told the lady that she had seen the ghost of the landlord's daughter and explained the legend. She replied that until then she had known nothing about it.'

Mr Davis added that he had heard of another ghostly happening at The George.

159

'In the course of writing my thesis, I went to Northampton to visit a man who had been in charge of The George two landlords ago, if you see what I mean,' he said. 'During our conversation, he told me his wife had often claimed that she heard mysterious footsteps – sounds made by invisible feet. He had pooh-poohed this until he had a frightening experience himself.

'One night after the bar had been closed, the barman went down into the cellar alone to tap the bungs back into the barrels from which beer had been drawn during the evening. The man then returned from the cellar and the door was locked. About twenty seconds later both men distinctly heard the barrels being tapped again. They knew that too much time had elapsed for the taps to be an echo. Both were too frightened to go down into the cellar to investigate.

'This made such an impression on the landlord that twenty years later, when he was telling me about it, he grew quite agitated.'

Whether it was because of the death of Sergeant Hobson, or whether the crazed girl painted tear-drops on the wall of her room for some unknown man, the decorated wall at the George Hotel remains a poignant memorial to some mysterious sorrow from the past.

THE LANGSTONE ARMS
(Kingham. Map reference: 98)

The Langstone Arms is a large building of Cotswold stone with a series of amazingly tall brick chimneys rising decoratively above its roof. Situated in a commanding position on the road which runs from the Oxfordshire village of Kingham to Kingham Station, its windows have one of the finest views of unspoilt countryside that any inn could wish for.

'This place is about 170 years old,' explained the landlord, Sidney Scales. 'I think it was originally built for the squire of Langstone, although they say its foundations are much earlier. In fact, there is a strong local theory that our cellars were once connected to nearby Bruern Abbey by a subterranean passage. There are some strange features about the cellars – where, incidentally, we have our well – such as a door that seems to lead to nowhere, and a bricked up archway which could have been the entrance to a tunnel.'

Perhaps it was this rumoured connection with a religious establishment which gave rise to the belief that the phantom which haunts the Langstone Arms is a nun, although Mr Scales doubts this very much.

'I don't think anyone can really say what it is,' he said. 'It has been described as a faintly luminous shape about the size of a man, but too vague to have any features. A few years ago it was exorcised by the vicar of Rissington Church, but I don't think the ceremony was all that successful. Strange things still happen here.'

An example of this had occurred a few days before I visited the inn when the barman, Steve Palmer, was gripped with an inexplicable sensation of fear one night after closing time.

'I don't believe in ghosts, but . . .' said Mr Palmer. 'Well, I didn't believe in them . . . Anyway, this night everything was the same as any other night. I came out of the kitchen after the bars had closed and went up the stairs to the corridor which leads to my room. As you can see, this is a rambling place and I had quite a distance to go. I must have been halfway there when suddenly it happened.

'I was seized by a sensation of terror such as I have never experienced before in my life. I don't know what it was or what caused it, but I was rooted to the spot. I said to myself, "I'm not going on any further." It got better when I came downstairs again.'

Mr Palmer had only just taken up his job at the inn, and the sensation might have been the ghost's way of making him aware of its presence, a pattern of ghostly behaviour which is the accepted thing at several of England's haunted inns.

'You should have seen Steve the next day,' chuckled Mr Scales. 'He looked so bad I asked him what was the matter, and then he told me. But he's not the only one to have experienced something here. If dogs go near Room 1 – that's believed to be the haunted room – their hairs stand on end without reason.

'On one occasion several customers in the bar saw the white shape of the ghost glide along behind the bar and vanish through the wall.

'Another time, I was behind the bar serving a party of motorcar dealers and their wives when I looked up and saw something go past the window. I could see that it was not the usual outline of a human being, and I said, "What was that?" And as I spoke one of the women of the party collapsed to the floor in a faint. When she came round all she could say was that she had been terrified by "something" at the window.'

THE REINDEER
(Banbury. Map reference: 133)

Oliver Cromwell once held Parliament in this inn which is believed to be the oldest in Banbury. On that occasion some royalist officers were placed on trial in the Globe Room, and one of those prisoners has returned again and again to the inn as a 'phantom Cavalier figure' – Until the panelling of the Globe Room was sold to the Banbury Council to go in the Civic Centre, that is – from then on the haunting of the Reindeer ceased. It would be interesting to know whether in the dead of night when the building is deserted, the phantom Cavalier figure materialises by the old panelling in the Civic Centre.

THE WESTON MANOR HOTEL
(Weston-on-the-Green. Map reference: 161)

The Weston Manor Hotel is steeped in history. It was originally presented to Robert de Oilly by William the Conqueror as a reward for his services, later it became a monastery and after the Dissolution of the Monasteries it was used as a private residence. In 1589, after a legal wrangle over ownership, it was actually besieged by the Earl of Lincoln. During the Civil War, when Prince Rupert's cavalry was defeated at the Battle of Islip, the prince took refuge there.

The same night the victorious General Fairfax, commander of Cromwell's troops, quartered his men at Weston-on-the-Green and stayed at Weston Manor himself. It is said that he actually slept in the room where Rupert was hidden (according to legend he was crouching in the chimney). Early in the morning, when Fairfax was sleeping, the Prince crept out, put on the clothes of a dairymaid and thus disguised managed to escape to Oxford.

From then until after World War II the manor was in private hands, but shortly after the war it became a country club and then an hotel. According to Nicholas Price, the proprietor, the hotel has inherited at least two ghosts from the manor's colourful past.

'I have been here eight years and I am utterly convinced they exist,' he said. 'One is a phantom coach which comes through the yard at the back. Unfortunately, despite a lot of research and inquiries at the village, I have not been able to find out anything about the story that must lie behind it. All we know is that a coach drives through the yard and then just vanishes. We did have an elderly gardener from the village who was so "aware" of it that he would never cross the track it took but would always walk the long way round.

'Our other – and more famous – ghost is Mad Maude. She was a young nun who was executed here about five centuries ago.'

The bedroom haunted by Maude is the finest in the hotel, panelled with oak and boasting an ancient and very comfortable four-poster bed. The story goes that when the hotel was a monastery the young nun from a nearby convent fell in love with one of the monks and one fateful night she was discovered in her lover's cell.

Maude was tried and found guilty for her sin of breaking her chastity vow and for causing another to do likewise. No hint has come down through time as to the punishment meted out to her lover, or lovers. But this is hardly surprising as the woman took the burden of the blame for the sins of the flesh in those days, and the Church fathers gave a twist to the words of Saint Paul in his first Epistle to the Corinthians '. . . it is better to marry than to burn' by declaring it was better to burn than love. In the grounds of Weston Manor Maude was chained to a stake with faggots heaped around her and turned into a human torch as an example to wrongdoers.

There is no doubt in Nicholas Price's mind that the victim's ghost returns to the manor.

'There have been so many people who have seen or "felt" something that it could not be put down to imagination,' he said. 'We often have conferences and courses here and on one occasion I had arranged for the course leader to have the best room in the hotel. He arrived late and went straight up to his room and got into the four-poster without knowing the room was haunted or, indeed, anything about Mad Maude.'

At breakfast the next morning he came straight to Mr Price and demanded to have his room changed.

'He was white-faced and I gather that – not to put too fine a point on it – he had been very scared,' the proprietor explained. 'He said emphatically that if I could not give him another room he would stay at some other place in the neighbourhood and just come for the course during daylight. I asked him what was the matter – although I had already guessed – and he told me that in the night he had woken up with a terrible sense of dread. He was aware of a presence in the room, and with it was a sensation of menace, a heightened atmosphere of the abnormal. He could see nothing in the darkness, but he knew there was someone invisible there, and he was terrified.'

Mr Price has another version of the Mad Maude story: 'In the village they say the hotel is haunted by the phantom of a dairymaid who fell down the tower. Perhaps she committed suicide. At the bottom of the tower there is a wooden floor with a mark on it, and this is said to have been made by her blood. They say she haunts the tower, but personally, I think she is a different ghost. In which case the Weston Manor has three ghostly visitors.'

THE WHITE HART
(Minster Lovell. Map reference: 166)

The ghost of the White Hart is that of a tragic girl known as Rosalind. Wearing a veil, her misty figure has been glimpsed with her face in her hands as though weeping, and at times the sound of sobbing has accompanied this manifestation. According to a local tradition the unfortunate Rosalind was jilted by her lover and, while her mind was clouded by anguish, took her own life.

When the ghost has materialised it is always close to an old spiral staircase which used to lead to a loft where the suicide took place.

Salop

THE ACTON ARMS
(Morville. Map reference: 1)

One of the busiest pub ghosts in Britain must have been the white apparition which haunted Mrs Mary Walker, an employee of the Acton Arms. When I visited the small hotel she told me that she caught sight of it almost daily – and sometimes several times a day at that.

'The haunted room is upstairs,' she explained. 'I see the apparition when I go into it. It appears as a white shape, vaguely in the form of a man, and when I enter the room it seems to be sitting or crouching. But the moment I am in the room it whisks away.'

She showed me a long corridor upstairs with creaking floorboards and, whether it was the floorboards coupled with what she had told me, or whether in this case I was responsive to psychic influence I do not know, but I had a keener impression of the supernatural here than in any other haunted inn I have visited.

'Sometimes when I come along this passage I see him flit across it from one room to another,' Mrs Walker continued. 'It's like seeing a sheet flick from one door to the other. There is a story that once this place was connected to the church across the road by a tunnel, and the monk used it for some unlawful purpose – probably to meet a lady. Unfortunately no one seems to know the legend any longer, but the fact remains the ghost appears constantly.

'I have been seeing him for years now, and I am used to it. He is quite harmless.'

THE NAG'S HEAD
(Shrewsbury. Map reference: 106)

The ghostly coachman at the Nag's Head, one of Shrewsbury's oldest pubs, has earned the reputation of alarming landlords with a series of supernatural tricks. His activities reached a pitch early in 1982 following renovations which began in the previous year. Workmen opened a panelled room which had been sealed off for many years. The plan was to make a passage out of the room but when this was found to be impossible it was shut up again. It is believed that this was where a coachman hanged himself in the 18th century, and it seems that the builders' activities earned his displeasure.

In May, 1982, the *Shrewsbury Chronicle* reported how the landlord, Clive Preece, and his family were 'forced to sleep in their first floor living rooms with all the lights on because of the ghost'.

The reason for the quitting of the upstairs bedrooms was the sounds of stertorous breathing issuing from a sealed-up fireplace and mysterious crashing noises and footsteps. More uncomfortable was a freezing wind which blew through two of the bedrooms despite mild May weather outside.

'The wife of the previous landlord was frightened of the ghost,' said Peta Preece who, with her husband, moved into the pub at the end of 1981. 'She said the more she grew to dislike the place, the noisier the ghost became. She warned us of it before we moved in. I'm a sceptical type of person but after a few weeks I saw her again and discovered that what I had heard was exactly what she had been hearing.'

To add to the mystery of the Nag's Head there is an ill-omened picture painted on the inside of a cupboard door in one of the rooms where the ghost is active. The picture, of an allegorical figure, is said to have been the cause of a woman committing suicide by jumping out of the window – at least she was believed to have been gazing at it before taking her life, and it is still considered bad luck at the Nag's Head to look at it.

As far as is known, the coachman has only been seen once and this was by the young daughter of a previous licensee who kept asking her mother and father to tell her about 'the man in the funny long coat' who came through the wall.

Somerset

THE CASTLE HOTEL
(Taunton. Map reference: 36)

Taunton Castle has several paranormal manifestations to its credit, two of them being aural in nature. The castle, which was built on the site of a Saxon earthwork fortification in the 12th century, now houses the Taunton Museum and the Castle Hotel. It is in the latter that the wild strains of a fiddle have woken some guests staying in the Fiddler's Room. In the museum section of the castle visitors have heard a tramping sound as though made by the boots of invisible soldiers. Both phenomena are thought to go back to the time of the Monmouth Rebellion, which left a remarkable number of ghosts in its wake.

On 20 June, 1685, the Duke of Monmouth – the natural son of Charles II and Lucy Walter – was proclaimed James II by his Protestant adherents at Taunton. That night his lieutenants celebrated the occasion with a revel at the castle. Ladies faithful to the pretender's cause, danced with the officers who called for madder music and stronger wine. It was the last time they were to celebrate, because a few days later the duke attempted to surprise a 2,700-strong royal army on Sedgemoor, his own peasant force being just a hundred less than that number.

Cannon cut ghastly avenues through the ranks of the untrained rebels, and soon the attack became a rout. Two days later the duke was caught near Ringwood and taken before his uncle, King James, where he grovelled at the royal feet and even offered to become a Roman Catholic in return for a pardon. The king, having rather enjoyed this spectacle, sent him to the Tower where he was beheaded on 15 July.

This was not enough for James who decided to make a terrible example of all those who had supported the duke in his attempt to usurp him, and for the instrument of his revenge he chose Judge Jeffreys, first Baron of Wem.

In Taunton Jeffreys conducted the Bloody Assize in the Great Hall of the Castle, sentencing over two hundred local men to the gallows and condemning many more to be sold into slavery. The women who, such a short while ago, had danced gaily with Monmouth's lieutenants were whipped.

Now the music in the Fiddler's Room is thought to go back to the night of the duke's proclamation – the tramp of feet is that of the soldiers who dragged the rebels to face the wrath of the Hanging Judge. Two visible ghosts also haunt Taunton Castle. One is a man dressed as a cavalier and holding a pistol who appears on a certain landing. The other is a young lady dressed in the fashion popular at the time of Monmouth's Rebellion.

THE CHOUGHS
(Chard. Map reference: 42)

The Choughs is an old stone building which probably dates back to the Great Fire of Chard in 1577. When I visited it the landlord Bill Peters told me how he had found a clue to the inn's haunting when he removed a false wall and found the original wall further back with a tombstone incorporated into it. Both he and his wife Verity said that they had experienced supernatural manifestations.

'One morning I was wiping the glasses in the back bar at about ten o'clock, and someone went up the corridor and I said to my husband, "A little old lady has gone up the corridor," ' said Verity.

'He said, "No – it's the ghost."

' "Don't be so silly," I said and ran down the passage to the back door, but there was nothing there. Yet something *had* gone down the corridor and, as we were talking, the back door gave a bang as though someone had slammed it. We looked everywhere, but there was nothing in the place. We hadn't even opened the pub.

'If you stand behind the bar and you look into the corridor you sometimes seem to see a shadowy form – you know how it is when you see something out of the corner of your eye and you're not sure what it is. Some nights you can see it going up and down, up and down. This does not happen regularly, but every so often this shadow is busy in the corridor.

'I think it is related to Winifred's tombstone in the wall. She may be upset because it is upside down and can't rest because of that.

'On one occasion there was this activity in the corridor and I said to Bill, "I'm not imagining this. You look, too, and if you see anything, knock!" He agreed, and soon afterwards we knocked on the counter simultaneously, which proved that it was not just one of us seeing the ghost.

'Strange things happen in the bar, too. Pint pots have jumped off the shelves for no reason at all and not broken when they landed, it was as though something invisible carried them. There was a gentleman sitting in the bar one day and his Guinness was swiped right off the counter. He said, "I've had enough – I'm off," and he was. But the glass didn't break.'

I was told of other strange happenings. For example, a lady who stayed in one of the rooms in the morning complained some force had thrown her from her bed.

There is a more sinister story which Bill Peters confirmed. Before World War II a visitor was haunted in the night by the sounds of female laughter and a menacing male voice. In the morning he left abruptly with a strange mark across his face as though he had been struck with a whip.

THE HOLMAN CLAVEL
(Blagdon. Map reference: 83)

A pub with the strange name of Holman Clavel stands by itself on a road not far from the village of Blagdon, in the Blackdown Hills. It is haunted by the spirit of a monk who enjoys playing tricks on the hotel staff and indulging in midnight games of skittles.

The landlord, John Clapp, explained that the unusual name Holman Clavel comes from old English words, *helme* meaning holly and *clavel* meaning a recess. It is thought that the holmans were men who cut holly trees on a nearby hill. When their day's work was over it is probable they would enjoy their beer or cider in the inn's inglenook. Therefore the Holman Clavel means a place where the holly cutters relaxed by the fire. It is six hundred years old and was a resting place for the monks on their pilgrimages to Glastonbury Abbey, and today it is unique in that it is owned by the local parish council.

It is believed that the ghost which attached itself to the Holman Clavel is that of a defrocked monk. Over the generations he has been nicknamed Charlie, and it is agreed he is a friendly ghost. In the days when cider was served from jugs he was often blamed for mysteriously emptying them . . .

Like some other ghosts mentioned in this book, Charlie enjoys playing pranks. 'Things disappear and then turn up months and months later,' Mr Clapp said. 'Once the key of a box disappeared. It was missing for two or three years and then one morning there it was, right in the middle of the carpet on the floor of the bar.'

He tells a story of a cameraman who came to film the Holman Clavel for a television programme. When he had finished, he afterwards said, he was one hundred per cent sure he had locked up all his equipment in the boot of his car before leaving the inn that evening. Yet when he got home he found he did not have his camera or a single piece of his gear. It was found standing in the centre of the car park when he came back the following day.

As to the actual haunting by Charlie, Mr Clapp said that one of the members of the local radio station had an experience in 1970. He knew nothing whatsoever about Charlie as he had just arrived. He swore that one night he heard a noise and there was someone – and he described the figure as that of a monk, in a long flowing gown – appearing to float in the corner. He admitted he was petrified but, moments later, managed to jump out of bed and switch on the light. When he did so he saw nothing.

The Holman Clavel has a very fine old skittle alley. Apparently two American residents, a writer and his wife, came down one morning, and the girl said, 'They were playing bowls late last night, weren't they?'

Vi, Mr Clapp's wife, said, 'Yes, I expect so.'

The bowling alley runs behind the bedroom in which the Americans had been sleeping. The rumble of the heavy wooden ball, as it went down the alley to the ninepins, would have been easy for them to hear.

Mrs Clapp thought for a minute and then said, 'But there wasn't anyone out in the skittle alley last night.' Her husband agreed there wasn't, so she asked the American girl, 'What time was this?'

'It must have been one or two o'clock,' the girl replied.

Mr Clapp said he and his wife told her no one could have been playing at that time.

'But I heard bowls going down that alley,' said the girl emphatically, still sticking to her story when it was proved beyond doubt that no human being could have been playing skittles.

'Of course that wasn't the first time,' said Mr Clapp. 'Several people who have stayed here recently said they have heard the balls going down the alley late at night when the pub has been closed.'

To introduce a personal note, I believe I became one of Charlie's victims when I arranged to photograph the skittle alley where he is heard playing his midnight games. I asked John Clapp to pose with a ball at the bowling end while I went down on one knee with my Rolleiflex at a spot well to one side.

'Send down a ball so we can have an action shot,' I called out. Mr Clapp obliged, bowling the six pound sphere of *lignum vitae* down the opposite side of the alley so that he would not skittle me as I held up my electronic flash. The landlord was an expert bowler and the ball should have missed me easily, but as I watched it in the viewfinder I saw it suddenly change direction as though deflected by an invisible hand. It did not swerve but altered course at an angle and, before I could move, struck my right kneecap with an agonising impact. It was several days before I could walk properly again, and today, several years afterwards, I am painfully reminded of the phantom monk when I go up or down stairs.

Was this the penalty I had to pay for invading his privacy with my camera?

THE PLOUGH
(Holford. Map reference: 123)

The legend behind The Plough has all the ingredients of a traditional ghost story – a foul murder, hidden gold and the return of the spectral victim. It stands at Holford, close to Bridgwater Bay, a white building roofed with mellow red tiles which remind one of Provence. Peter Fry, who became the landlord after his retirement from the RAF, told me that the inn had been built in 1430.

On one wall he showed me a poster which had been pasted up three centuries ago and then covered over with wallpaper. The printing can still be deciphered and proclaims that Joseph Thistle was anxious to form a 'clock and watch club'.

'The legend concerns the murder of a Spanish traveller who stayed here a long time ago,' explained Mr Fry. 'He was a merchant on his way to Bristol, and it was believed that he was carrying a lot of gold coins with him. When he left his room and came down the outside stairs he was attacked and killed by an unknown person or persons. It was not the landlord, by the way, but robbers who had followed the unfortunate stranger until they could seize their chance.

'As soon as he was dead, they broke into his room, but they found nothing. The Spaniard had been too smart, he had hidden his money and to this day it has not been found. The most popular belief was that he buried it in the inn grounds. After his death his ghost was seen to return to the scene of his murder, and people got the idea that he was making sure that his property remained safely in its hiding place.'

Mr Fry added that the ghost only appeared at The Plough during the month of November.

'I have not seen him myself,' he continued, 'but my wife and daughter have. At first he was supposed to have appeared on the stairs where he was killed, but when they were dismantled to make way for the back extension, he transferred to an upstairs room. And that's where my wife saw him – a dark cloaked figure which, after a few moments, just vanished. The strange thing was that she did not feel at all scared. Twelve months later my daughter had exactly the same experience.'

173

Staffordshire

THE LEOPARD INN
(Burton-on-Trent. Map reference: 100)

When Ken and Rose Cooter gave up the licence of The Leopard in November, 1979, their account of the haunting of the pub was given prominence in the *Burton Daily Mail*. Five years earlier when they took over the Leopard Inn the previous landlady warned them that she frequently heard a sound like the rustle of a skirt in the cellar passage.

'I was getting some bottles out of the cellar and I heard the same noises,' said Mrs Cooter. 'I looked outside and there was nothing there at all, so I thought maybe I had imagined it.'

Ten minutes later her husband was talking to two guests in the bar when he became aware of the rustling.

'He heard the swishing of skirts and as he turned he thought he saw somebody in the lounge,' Mrs Cooter continued. 'It was like a figure passing the bar, but when he put the lights on nothing was there.'

After this initial experience the Cooters heard the mysterious sounds on several occasions during the following years, though no explanation for them was ever found.

THE SEIGHFORD HALL HOTEL
(Seighford. Map reference: 145)

When this Elizabethan mansion became a hotel the proprietors not only inherited a wealth of historical tradition but a delightful ghost who at times has acted as an unofficial baby-sitter. It is said that if children stay in room No 8 she sometimes appears to see that they are all right and run her hand gently over their foreheads. A hotel brochure explains: 'Seighford even had a friendly ghost, a governess who returned whenever a new governess was appointed.'

The story goes back two centuries to when the Elde family engaged a young governess who, before long, fell passionately in love with the father of her charges. It appears that he returned the girl's ardour – until his wife found out. When their affair became known he renounced her and this, coupled with the weight of the scandal, caused the governess to commit suicide.

Since then her spirit returned on many occasions to Seighford Hall. Some believe that she was searching for the children whom she looked after long ago. Another tradition says that when a new governess was appointed to the household the ghost would look her over. On her first night the newcomer would hear footsteps on the stairs which led up to the small room allotted to the governesses, the door would slowly open and a dark figure would appear. She would bend over the new governess for a long moment and then melt away as though satisfied that she was suitable for the post which she had held long ago.

Suffolk

THE BULL
(Long Melford. Map reference: 31)

Long Melford is surrounded by majestic sweeps of parkland dotted here and there with great manors, many of which date back to Tudor times. Its main street is dominated by a long timber-framed hotel named The Bull which is a Mecca for ghost-hunting societies. It was built in 1450 by a rich wool merchant when the town was the centre of the profitable cloth industry.

In the 16th century it became an inn and, later, when coaches used to clatter into town with their horns echoing, it was used as a posting house. A relic of those days is to be seen in the inn's courtyard where there is still part of the original coaching gallery. The inside of The Bull is as picturesque as its exterior and in the pleasant lounge, beams five centuries old support the ceiling. One carries the carving of a 'woodwose', or wild man, which was a mysterious forest-being often depicted in medieval decoration.

The reason for the ghost-hunters' interest in The Bull is that in 1648 a yeoman named Richard Everard was murdered by one Roger Greene in the inn's hallway. The haunting which from time to time manifests itself at The Bull is attributed to this crime and takes the form of poltergeist activity. For example, the massive old oaken door which leads from the hall to the dining room has been known to swing open by itself on many occasions. In the past a head waiter at The Bull has declared that on several occasions he has witnessed various objects suddenly fly right across the dining-room. Once he had to duck when a copper jug was hurled at him by an invisible force.

Among other incidents which have occurred without explanation is the mysterious moving of chairs in the dining-room. Although they have been left in their usual places

176

in the evening, in the morning they have been found grouped in a semi-circle round the fireplace. There has never been any reason why any member of the hotel staff would want to get up in the middle of the night and re-position the furniture.

Colonel Dawson, a previous landlord, reported hearing footsteps pass his bedroom door but, when he got up to investigate, he found the corridor empty. Far from content with this state of affairs, he brought his dogs upstairs to continue the search. As soon as they reached the passage, they refused to advance another step and crouched trembling with terror.

On another occasion a guest heard footsteps outside her bedroom early one morning, followed by a rap at the door. Thinking it was a maid bringing an early cup of tea, she called out: 'Come in, please!' Her words were followed by a resounding crash, as though the tray with the tea things had been dropped to the floor. The guest left her bed and opened the door with the idea of helping the maid to pick up the shattered crockery but, to her amazement, she found no one there nor any sign of broken china.

THE CROWN
(Bildeston. Map reference: 46)

The Crown was built as the home of a wealthy wool merchant in 1495. In those days Bildeston, in common with many West Suffolk villages (of which nearby Lavenham is the most splendid), was prospering from the booming wool trade. Rich half-timbered houses are still to be seen as monuments to this bygone affluence.

The Crown is the oldest inn in the village, and is historically interesting because, in the middle of the 17th century, its proprietor had his own coinage struck. The Crown coins were actually trade tokens which were issued to customers because of the drastic shortage of small change in England at that time.

With a history stretching over almost five centuries, it is not surprising that The Crown has the reputation of being a haunted inn. Although the reason for this is long forgotten, supernatural manifestations are said to be ghostly footsteps and unexplained hammering sounds. On one occasion some years ago, a landlord thought local lads were having a game with him by banging on the front door. He ran upstairs to a window to see who the culprits were but on poking his head out saw that the street was deserted – yet the mysterious knocking continued all the while.

Another phenomenon reported in the past is of people being touched by invisible fingers, said to be as cold as ice. Perhaps the skeleton which was once found in a priesthole behind the lounge bar fireplace has some connection with the mysterious manifestations.

According to the landlord, Kevin Broome, the inn has four actual ghosts.

'There is a maidservant dressed in grey, who haunts the courtyard and stable where she hanged herself,' he said. 'There's an old man in a three-cornered hat who sits in the lounge bar, and two children in Victorian dress who roam the inn holding a musical box. They have been seen on a couple of occasions since I came here a year ago by customers who are quite sober, sensible people. And once a customer returned to the bar as white as a sheet. He told me he was about to pop into the gents in the courtyard when someone opened the door for him. When he got inside there was no one there. He was petrified.'

I first visited The Crown ten years ago as a journalist seeking supernatural stories and the then landlord, Len Faiers, told me how his mother-in-law had experienced something 'very queer' in an upstairs room. She had been sitting at her dressing table when she glanced in the mirror and saw a reflection which she described as a 'strange shape'. When she turned to see the cause of the reflection the room was empty.

But any legend which could explain this odd and frightening occurrence – as with the sounds and touchings – has been lost with the passage of time.

On 25 June 1966, there was a local newspaper story on how Tom Corbett, the noted clairvoyant, visited The Crown with a reporter and press photographer. After he had told them about the psychic atmosphere of the inn he left for his nearby home. The two newspaper men stayed in one of The Crown's double rooms. During the night they were awakened by loud mysterious footsteps in the corridor outside. They ventured out of their room only to find the passage empty. When they nervously returned to their room they began shivering because of a dramatic and unaccountable drop in the temperature.

THE QUEEN'S HEAD
(Blyford. Map reference: 128)

It was the discovery of an old smugglers' tunnel which triggered off a series of queer events at the Queen's Head some years ago. There is a legend in Blyford that local freetraders used to hide their contraband in the village church, and that it found its way there via an underground passage from the inn. When renovations were carried out at the pub a bricked-up tunnel was found in the cellar which gave weight to the story. The same renovations had the effect of causing paranormal disturbances.

The most dramatic of these occurred when there was a crowd of regulars in the bar. Suddenly they stopped talking and glasses were held half-raised as the sound of heavy footfalls came from the ceiling. The landlord and his wife knew of no one who should be in the rooms above them and there could only be one explanation for the noise – a burglar.

Among the customers were two off-duty policemen who ran upstairs hoping to make an arrest, but they found no one. Everything was secure and as they finally returned to the bar the conversation turned to other unexplained things which had happened since the entrance to the tunnel had been uncovered. From time to time the landlord heard disembodied noises, sometimes loud like a series of explosions and sometimes like the sound of wood snapping.

These aural manifestations had also been heard by his wife and some of the customers, and it was speculated that they might be supernatural echoes of smugglers at work with barrels and cases.

Surrey

THE ANGEL
(Guildford. Map reference: 3)

One of the most mysterious forms of haunting to take place in an English inn was reported in the *Surrey Advertiser* of 27 February 1970. The scene of the visitation was Guildford's Angel Hotel which is situated halfway down the old cobbled High Street. This one-time posting house would make an ideal setting for any ghost story, having been built on old monastic foundations which gave it a 13th century crypt which may once have been used to store the wines of Henry III.

The name of the inn came from a statue of the flying angel which was placed on a cross in the High Street by the White Friars of Guildford in 1345. Another hint of its clerical connections came in 1951 with the discovery, during renovations, of a small 14th century metal lion which was thought to represent the Lion of St Mark. In 1827 The Angel was 'one of the very faire innes' mentioned by John Taylor, the Water Poet. In the same century, the Times Coach left the inn regularly for Charing Cross via Epsom. The Prince Imperial of France stayed at The Angel in 1876, giving his name to the room where a phantom made a thirty-minute appearance in a looking glass.

On the evening of 30 January, 1970, Mr and Mrs C. Dell, of Bayswater, were staying in Room 1. The following day Mr Dell told the manager of The Angel how he had awakened in the night and, looking at the bedroom mirror which measured seven feet by four feet, saw the image of a man in a military uniform. He was so intrigued that he crossed the room to look closer and saw that the spectre, which was visible in the glass from the waist up, was that of a rather striking-looking man with a sweeping 'bandit' moustache. The uniform could have been that of a Continental soldier of the last century.

Mr Dell called his wife. At first she could only see her own reflection in the mirror, but after five minutes she was able to see it exactly as her husband described. Mr Dell was so intrigued by the apparition in the mirror that he took a ballpoint pen and, at 3 pm, began to sketch it. By the time the figure faded away it had been visible to the Dells for half an hour.

THE HOP BAG INN
(Farnham. Map reference: 84)

An inn haunted by a phantom coach is the Hop Bag at Farnham, Surrey, which stands in Downing Street, close to the large municipal car park. Gwen Harrison, the wife of landlord Bert Harrison, explained that the story went back to the 18th century when the Hop Bag (so called because of the hop gardens which used to be opposite) was a stopping point for the Winchester-London coach.

One cold winter night a young woman sat in the inn, straining her ears for the sounds of the horses which would herald the arrival of the midnight stage. When it finally rumbled into the yard, long overdue, the girl rushed out to meet it. In the dim lantern light the driver stumbled down from his box and announced there had been a hold-up between Winchester and Farnham.

The girl's fiancé, who had been a passenger on the coach, had resisted the masked road agents, and one had shot him dead with a pistol. Since then, until the inn was burnt down and rebuilt at the beginning of this century, the shadowy figure of the broken-hearted girl was often seen in the yard. Another ghostly echo of the tragic incident which still lingers is the sound of horses and the coach rumbling into the precincts of the pub.

Mrs Harrison declares that on several occasions her youngest daughter has sworn she heard the sound of horses in the night, while she herself heard strange noises usually around 2.30 am but always she found the bar empty and nothing unusual to be seen.

Guests at the Hop Bag have had the same experience of hearing sounds – sounds which could reflect the bustle of a coach arrival – but when they have looked into the yard they have found it deserted.

THE MARQUIS OF GRANBY
(Esher. Map reference: 103)

My mind was full of Charles Dickens as I approached the Marquis of Granby which stands on the A3 close to those oddly named traffic roundabouts, the Scilly Isles. It was here that Samuel Weller beheld his mother-in-law on his pilgrimage to Dorking in Chapter 27 of *Pickwick Papers*. Dickens was a connoisseur of inns and it is obvious that he had affection for the inn which he described thus:

'The Marquis of Granby, in Mrs Weller's time, was quite a model of a roadside public house of the better class – just large enough to be convenient, and small enough to be snug. On the opposite side of the road was a large sign-board on a high post, representing the head and shoulders of a gentleman with an apoplectic countenance, in a red coat with deep blue facings, and a touch of the same blue over his three-cornered hat, for a sky. Over that again were a pair of flags; beneath the last button of his coat were a couple of cannon; and the whole formed an expressive and undoubted likeness of the Marquis of Granby of glorious memory.'

Dickens had a keen instinct for a ghost story but he missed the fact that the Marquis was haunted – perhaps it had not begun in his time. At the pub I was told that the previous landlord, who had been there for many years, had – along with his family – frequently heard footsteps and the rustling of a long skirt upstairs. Who this unseen lady was and why she should return to the pub is not known, but it is possible that she was connected with the mysterious cupboard which has a strong Dickensian flavour.

It is always kept locked and I was told that the staff regarded it with a sort of horror though, like the ghost, no one could explain why. The previous landlord regarded it as an area of particular evil and to protect the pub and its people kept a huge Bible propped against the door.

Tyne and Wear

THE GROTTO
(Marsden. Map reference: 78)

England's most unusual pub must be The Grotto. It is unusual because apart from being haunted by a thirsty ghost, it is set in caverns at the bottom of 112-foot cliffs of light-coloured Dolomite limestone. In the old days, visitors to The Grotto had to walk along the beach or toil down Jack the Blaster's stairs, but today they can descend in forty seconds by means of an electric lift to the modern building which fronts the ancient, sea-worn caves once used by smugglers.

The first person to use The Grotto caves for a purpose other than smuggling was an Allenhead miner known as Jack the Blaster. In 1782 he came to work in the Marsden quarries. When he and his wife found the rents in South Shields too high, they moved into the caves to live. To reach the caves more easily he cut steps in the cliff and soon he and his family were one of the curiosities of the neighbourhood. Sightseers came from all over the district to see the troglodytes. The Blaster was quick to cash in on the interest. He enlarged the caves and began selling ale, and so The Grotto began its life as an inn. Its first landlord died comparatively wealthy after living there for ten years.

When I visited the subterranean pub in search of the story of the ghost known as Jack the Jibber, the landlord was a pleasant Australian named Jim Lofthouse who showed me a Georgian pewter tankard from which the phantom had been said to quench his supernatural thirst.

'If the beer is left in anything but this particular tankard he won't touch it,' Mr Lofthouse said. 'And it has been known for people who have drunk from it to have it knocked from their lips. Sometimes when we come here in the morning the place looks as though a tornado has struck it. Chairs knocked over and all that sort of thing. Then at night we leave the tankard full of beer on the bar and everything is peaceful again. It's a sort of offering to the ghost of the smuggler who died here, though how a spirit can consume beer I don't understand.'

'Another thing about Jack the Jibber is that he hates flowers,' said the landlord's wife, Esme Lofthouse. 'As soon as I bring any in here they wither and die.'

This story of the thirsty ghost was first told, as far as I can ascertain, in *Chambers' Journal* in 1875:

> A certain noted smuggler had arranged for a lugger to discharge its cargo here. As the time arrived at night that the vessel ought to be approaching the coast, and a signal shown from the cave to indicate safety, a man long suspected of treachery was missing. The smuggler, therefore, to warn the skipper to keep away, set his dogs barking and let off his gun, which brought the coastguard down (who turned out to be close by) but who were told by the smuggler that thieves had attempted to enter the hut. The skipper, taking the hint, had sheered off . . .
>
> The story would not be complete without its touch of horror. For years after, moans were heard to proceed from this hole in the cliff, and no one would approach it after nightfall. The cause assigned for these lamentations was that the smuggler who attempted to betray the gang, being caught, was placed in a tub, and hauled up by a rope under the pole, and only let down once a day to receive some scant food and the gibes of his mates, his situation being rendered yet more cruel from his position permitting him to witness his comrades feasting and being made a target for the refuse of their festivities.

Finally the gang quit the cave. Perhaps the vigilance of excisemen had caused them to flee the district, or perhaps they had finally decided that death was to be the punishment for the traitor. One can imagine the growing terror felt by the prisoner when a day passed and his old companions did not return to the cave. As the black hours dragged by, how he must have longed to hear the sound of seaboots on rough stone. Even their taunts and abuse would have been welcome now as his throat began to dry with thirst. Often he must have looked over the edge of his

184

swinging tub into the darkness below and wondered if it would be worth throwing himself over the side. But he knew that to do so would be suicide, he was too high up and the rock floor below would smash his body.

Finally thirst released him from his terrible torment, but his anguish and the agonising desire for drink have in some strange way remained with his ghost in the caverns of The Grotto.

West Midlands

THE BULL'S HEAD
(Meridan. Map reference: 32)

This 15th century inn is a stopping place for a phantom coach which sank with its driver into a mire when its horses bolted and left the road. It is said to travel on this old coach route from another inn, the appropriately-named Phantom Coach (see below). Apart from the sound of invisible wheels on the forecourt, the Bull's Head has a resident ghost. When I spoke to landlord Alan Wall he had only just taken over and had not yet experienced any paranormal manifestations himself, though he had already heard about the extra waiter.

'Apparently the poor chap hanged himself from one of our balconies years and years ago,' he said. 'He was a waiter here. I understand the staff have not minded him, they gave him the nickname of Fred.'

THE PHANTOM COACH
(Canley, Coventry. Map reference: 122)

'This inn is haunted all right,' landlord Hugh Curley told me. 'In the last eighteen months we have had two experiences.'

Although the pub is named after a phantom coach, the actual ghost who revisits the premises is believed to be the driver of that ill-fated vehicle, and he is known to the staff as Fred. Mr Curley explained that although the present building is only fifty years old, it was constructed on the site of an inn which went back centuries, and before the advent of the railways was a well-known coaching inn. Here paused the coach which made a regular journey from London to Holyhead.

'The old coaching road runs between Coventry and Meridan, and then goes on to Birmingham,' Mr Curley said.

'After this pub, the next stopping place was the Bull's Head at Meridan. In the coaching days it was all marshland round here, and on one occasion a team of horses bolted, dragging the coach off the road. It vanished into the swamp along with its driver.'

He said that Fred the driver manifests himself through the sound of his footsteps.

'It's just like somebody invisible walking past you,' he said. 'We were a little perturbed at first but we've got used to living with him now. As well as Fred, rumour has it that there is actually a phantom coach.'

Although the landlord has not witnessed it himself, there are local stories of it being seen on the road near the pub late at night, swaying wildly as the driver frantically tries to rein up his panic-stricken horses. It is a phenomenon which the pub shares with the Bull's Head at Meridan, which appears on the opposite page. Here there have been reports of the sound of a coach's iron-shod wheels rumbling up to the ancient inn. The fascinating thing about this aural manifestation is that it is easily recognisable as wheels rolling on cobblestones – and today the forecourt of the Bull's Head is covered with tarmacadam.

THE WHITE HART
(Caldmore Green, Walsall. Map reference: 164)

A popular piece of Victorian mythology concerned The Hand of Glory. Immortalised in *The Ingoldsby Legends*, it was a grisly candelabrum used to bewitch households into deep slumber and illuminate the burglarious activities which followed. The arm of a child, or the hand of a hanged felon, was pickled and treated with witches' unguents, then a candle was placed in its grasp and it was ready to cast its spell – and its unholy light – as soon as the wick was lit. Some accounts suggest the actual fingertips were lit.

Interest in this macabre subject was revived when a child's withered arm was discovered in the long-neglected attic of the White Hart Inn at Caldmore Green. Today the same arm can be seen in a special glass case at the Walsall Museum, complete with explanations of The Hand of Glory rite.

It is very doubtful if the mummified relic was ever used for magical purposes, yet the mystery of how it came to be hidden away in the inn has never been solved. One thing certain in the minds of many of the White Hart's customers is that the place where it was found is haunted.

'People around here all believe we have a ghost,' said landlady Mrs Heather Singh. 'We have heard all sorts of queer stories about it. Originally the building was a Tudor manor house, and it has had several opportunities to become haunted. During the Civil War a Mr Menzies was murdered here by the Roundheads. Another murder was committed in the loft later on, and at the beginning of this century a servant woman committed suicide up there.

'A previous landlady woke up one night and saw a white shape standing by her bed, and there have been plenty of reports of strange bumping sounds. One day my son had to go down into the cellar, and when he reached the end of it the lights went out. He groped his way back to the door and was just about to reach out for the switch when they came on again. Thinking it was a brief power failure he walked to the end again and, once more, the lights went off.

'This happened a third time, and then, as he stood in the dark, he felt something tap him on the shoulder. When the lights went on again there was nobody there.'

The most interesting case of haunting at the White Hart seems to relate to the mysterious arm. Some years ago a landlord there heard the sound of sobs coming from the disused attic where it had been found. He was greatly mystified, as the whole top storey had not been used for years, and went up to investigate. When he entered the attic he found it empty with the dust on the floor undisturbed. But in the centre of the room stood an old table which attracted his attention. Quite clearly imprinted in the dust which covered it was the mark of a child's hand.

West Sussex

THE ROYAL OAK
(East Lavant. Map reference: 140)

According to Wilfrid Miles, the landlord of the Royal Oak, the haunting of the pub was connected with an old grandfather clock which stood in the premises when he took over.

'Until it happened I was very sceptical about such things,' said Mr Miles, 'but we had experience of this phenomenon before we heard the local stories, so we must believe it.'

When the Miles family moved into the Royal Oak, the elder of their two young sons was fascinated by the clock, a Rapson made by the famous old firm of Chichester clockmakers. The boy cleaned the parts and tinkered with it until its heavy tick once more was heard in the inn. Almost immediately the two boys, who slept in an upstairs room, began to complain to their parents that something was coming into their room at night.

'At first I did not believe them,' Mr Miles said. 'I thought they were up to some sort of lark. But I got worried when sometimes I went into their room and found one of the boys had woken up in a state of terror.

'Then one night – soon after the clock had started again – I saw an apparition. I had got up at about one o'clock in the morning to go to the bathroom, and as I walked down the corridor, I saw a male figure – a slim, slightly misty figure with a very full beard. It was dressed in old-fashioned clothing and appeared as though it had just come from the boys' room. It was a most shattering experience.

'I could see it quite clearly but when I blinked it vanished. I then questioned my sons very carefully about what had been going on in their room, and they told me they had seen a figure sitting at the end of their bed.'

Mr Miles was convinced this apparition had some mysterious connection with the clock. Soon after his experience, the

189

wife of an old friend came to stay at the Royal Oak. She had known it before the Miles had come there.

'Do you know it's haunted?' she asked.

'I asked her where the ghost was supposed to appear,' said Mr Miles, 'and she pointed up to the room where the boys slept. Later I heard a rumour that someone had died in very mysterious circumstances up there.'

After the visitation Mr Miles stopped the grandfather clock and would not have it started up again in the Royal Oak.

Mrs Doris Miles added that, although she had never seen the apparition herself, both she and her husband have often heard heavy footsteps sounding on the ceiling above the bar when they have known there is nobody upstairs.

THE WHITE HORSE
(Storrington. Map reference: 168)

When Mike and Linda Balster moved into the White Horse at the end of 1978 they were soon aware that there was an extra guest at the hotel – a ghost who left a sensation of extreme cold in its wake.

Mrs Balster's first encounter with the entity was one evening when she was working in one of the upstairs bedrooms. As she bent over a wash basin she felt a touch on her shoulder. Thinking it was her husband she turned, and was confronted with an empty room.

'I heard footsteps and the whole room went like a fridge,' she told the press later. 'I raced down to the bar terrified. Mike didn't believe me. I wouldn't go upstairs for the rest of the evening – I sat in the office for three hours.'

Later she became used to the presence when she was working upstairs, and the wife of the previous landlord admitted that she had been troubled by the ghost but had not mentioned it to the Balsters as she and her husband did not want to alarm them. She said that when she was using a vacuum-cleaner upstairs the ghost would actually shake her.

There was some speculation that the spirit might be that of Sir Arnold Bax, a former master of the King's Music, who stayed at the White Horse between 1940 and 1953 when he died. But when a woman, who claimed to be psychic, stayed at the White Horse she believed the ghost went much farther back.

'She felt that the ghost was not that of Sir Arnold Bax but a spirit from a much earlier century, searching for something – almost as if it had come back to look for its partner,' said Mrs Balster. It was frighteningly chilling but not evil, she thought.

'One man told us that years ago a man hanged himself here in the cellar. We looked down there but it seemed impossible because the ceiling was so low. Then we discovered that the structure of the place had been altered.'

West Yorkshire

THE BLUE BALL
(Soyland. Map reference: 25)

The frightened ghost which from time to time returns to the Blue Ball is known as Faith. She was a servant at this moorland pub in the 18th century when she became the victim of one of the most ruthless landlords in the history of British inns. He was called Iron Ned, and under him the Blue Ball became a rendezvous for highwaymen, footpads and similar unsavoury characters.

'The story is that when he was the landlord here he used to chase the serving wenches,' Tony Foster, the present licensee, told me. 'He was supposed to have formed a rape and pillage gang.'

Soon after Faith went to work at the Blue Ball she was seduced by Iron Ned, and when it became obvious that she was pregnant he murdered her by drowning her on the moors. At the time her death was officially put down as suicide, but the locals had no doubt that it was the work of the landlord. Although Mr Foster has not encountered any ghostly happenings, previous landlords have sworn to hearing Faith's footsteps – sounding as though she was involved in a struggle – in the room where Iron Ned used to sleep.

THE FLEECE
(Elland. Map reference: 65)

For several generations The Fleece was known as 'the inn with the bloody stairs', and as the haunt of a ghost who in life was known as Leathery Coit.

'He was a traveller who was brutally murdered in a room here a long time ago,' said the landlord John Clarkson. 'When the body was dragged downstairs it left a trail of blood on the wooden steps which no amount of scrubbing could erase. After that people began to see the ghost of Leathery Coit driving his carriage out of the inn barn late at night.'

An old description of the haunting, preserved in a frame at The Fleece, reads:

> Those who dared to watch might see an awful sight, for at midnight the doors of a large barn at the top of Westgate slowly opened without human agency, and there issued forth a travelling carriage with headless horses and headless coachman who drove furiously down Dog-lane to Old Earth, and thence returned. The coming of the spectral vision appears to have been usually accompanied by a sudden rush of wind, however quiet the night, and one can imagine how a sleeper, wakened suddenly by the violent gust or an unexpected noise, would listen, trembling, and say, 'There goes Leathery Coit'.

Joyce Clarkson, the wife of the landlord, described an odd incident which occurred at The Fleece.

'I was away and my husband was here on his own,' she said. 'He came into the bar and a customer told him he'd heard some one walking about upstairs, the sound of footsteps having come clearly through the ceiling. John dashed upstairs and searched the whole of the upper storey, but it was quite deserted.'

In July 1915, the *Halifax Courier* printed a startling news item about the phantom of The Fleece, which read:

> One night in the month of January, a man and a woman were returning home about midnight from the house of a sick relative, and, just as they reached the spot where the Railway Hotel now stands, there came a gust of wind, and Leathery Coit and his dreadful horses darted by while they clung to each other in terror.

THE OLD SILENT INN
(Near Stanbury. Map reference: 113)

The wonderfully-named Old Silent Inn stands in the heart of the Brontë country, just past the tiny village of Stanbury on the road which runs a mile east to Haworth. As one approaches, it is easy to imagine the figure of Heathcliffe stalking against the moor skyline.

The inn, made of solid, white-painted stone, blends perfectly with its wild setting which was made famous at the turn of the century by the historical novel *Ricroft of Withens* by Halliwell Sutcliffe. The most exciting part of the book centres round the Old Silent Inn and relates to the legend that Bonnie Prince Charlie had a hair's-breadth escape there.

When I stayed at the inn I learned from Mrs Brogan, wife of the then-proprietor, how it came to have such an unusual name.

'Originally it was called The Eagle because eagles used to fly in these parts,' she said. 'Then a traveller was murdered and thrown into a stream. The culprits were supposed to be a couple of Lancashire lads who fled to York after the deed. The local people were a highly independent lot in those days and they cared very little for authority. Therefore, when officers of the law came here to investigate the killing, no one would co-operate. In fact the whole district remained silent on the matter, and it was from this stubborn refusal to talk that the inn got its name.

'In the 18th century there was a whole clan of outlaws – the Carlesses – living in a valley nearby. They were nicknamed "The Lonely Folk" by the people of Stanbury, who greatly feared them because the young Carlesses used to carry off Stanbury girls. It was said that once a girl was abducted by the Lonely Folk she never wanted to return to her family. The inn used to be in the middle of a sort of no-man's-land between the village and Carless territory.'

According to local legend when Bonnie Prince Charlie was a fugitive with a price of £30,000 on his head, he took shelter at the Old Silent Inn. A rumour of his presence reached the Lonely Folk and one night they set out to capture him and earn the reward. In the nick of time the Pretender dropped through a trapdoor and into the saddle of his horse which had been kept harnessed in readiness for such an emergency.

The Prince's dramatic exit still delights Jacobite enthusiasts.

'We often have Americans turning up here asking to see the trapdoor,' Mrs Brogan said. 'The book by Sutcliffe is based on the Prince's stay here. Of course, there are all sorts of stories connected with an old place like this. The regulars will point to hollowed flags on the bar floor and tell you that they were worn by Timothy Feather's clog dancing. He was a tinker who used to live in the district ages ago and has become a sort of folk hero.'

The haunting of the inn has nothing to do with Bonnie Prince Charlie or Timothy Feather – it is a 'presence' which no one can account for. People often sense it, and a waitress at the inn told me that she was aware of it constantly. She added that it did not frighten her as the atmosphere at the inn (as anyone entering it can tell) is one of peace.

Mrs Brogan described the inn's other strange manifestation.

'I hear the sound of bells,' she said. 'They seem to tinkle in the distance – like fairy bells. When we first came here I was rather worried about them because, as you can imagine, I thought it was something peculiar happening to me. Then one day a new waitress started work here and, as I could hear them tinkling, she asked: "What are those little bells I can hear ringing?"

' "Thank goodness!" I said. "If you can hear them too, it's all right." '

Mrs Brogan knows of no explanation for the 'fairy' sound any more than the story behind the presence which some people sense at the inn. Could it be the two are connected?

'The tinkling does remind me a little of a bell which the previous landlady had,' she said thoughtfully. 'There are wildcats on the moors, and this old lady used to feed them. The ringing of the bell was to let them know when their food was ready.' Mrs Brogan smiled and added: 'If they were to stop, I'd really miss them – they're lovely.'

THE OLD TREE INN
(Kippax. Map reference: 115)

According to what landlord Albert Wright told the *Yorkshire Evening Post* in January, 1980, the Old Tree Inn has a rather extraordinary phantom.

'It's just a white haze with a smiling face,' Mr Wright said. 'I usually see it just before midnight when I am standing in the taproom. The ghost is at the corner of the music room bar. There is a sudden chill in the pub and I just freeze. I can't tell whether it's a man or a woman.'

The phenomenon has been seen by others including the husbands of two barmaids who work at the inn. One man glimpsed the hazy figure move past him on the cellar steps. The regulars of the pub think that the ghost is that of a previous landlord who was very attached to the Old Tree – so deeply attached in fact that he has remained on the premises despite the efforts of a vicar to exorcise him.

Wiltshire

THE CROWN INN
(Broad Hinton. Map reference: 52)

A ghost with a unique method of haunting was reported in the licensees' trade paper, the *Publican*, in December, 1979 – it tweaked people's ears.

'One of my customers had her ears tweaked three times,' Terry Kelley, the manager, was reported as saying. 'And each time she was on her way to the loo. Now she's afraid to go alone.' His wife Sally also became a victim of the phantom tweaker.

She had her right ear pulled suddenly while she was at work in the kitchen.

'I thought it was Terry and I turned round with the carving knife at the ready, but no one was there,' she said. 'It has happened to me since, but I immediately remembered the experiences of the previous victim.'

There is no known explanation for the ear-pulling by unseen fingers which usually took place towards closing time.

THE KING AND QUEEN
(Highworth. Map reference: 88)

A phantom monk glided into the headlines when it appeared late one night at The King and Queen. Not only did various newspapers cover the story, but the BBC paid a visit to the premises whose signboard shows a suitable pair of royal playing cards. The appearance was not dismissed as just another vague spook story because it was underlined by the landlord, Richard Nelms, taking out insurance worth £100,000 to protect his customers against supernatural shock.

'I thought of what might happen if any of my regulars saw the ghost,' he explained. 'They might panic, fall over and break their necks, or suffer heart attacks.' So Mr Nelms saw his insurance broker and arranged the cover.

There is a legend that the pub building once belonged to a monastery and had a passageway leading from its cellars to the crypt of the nearby church. This would certainly explain the nature of the spectre – a monk who, in the landlord's opinion, still seeks his lost love, a monk who might even have perished for the breaking of his chastity vows. He has not only been seen in the yard of The King and Queen, but has been glimpsed in other parts of Highworth, particularly in the local church. Here he has been seen on occasions by reputable townsfolk when they were alone in the old building, while a verger saw the dark-cowled figure quite frequently.

Describing his unnerving experience, Mr Nelms said, 'It was not long after I arrived. That particular evening I was alone in my bedroom with Tina, one of my Alsatian guard dogs, sleeping outside my door. For some reason she always likes to sleep there. Suddenly I heard her making a strange whimpering sound. I got up and found her trembling and looking down the passage. Then I was aware of footsteps although I could see no one there.'

Thinking that perhaps the sound came from outside the inn, he went down with Tina to the yard where his other Alsatian, Sheba, was in the dogs' compound. As he opened the yard door, he saw in the moonlight a figure standing motionless.

'I challenged him, and then let the dogs loose,' he continued. 'But strangely they refused to advance on what seemed to be a man in a long dark cloak. Then I knew it was no practical joker because he would have run from the dogs.

'I decided to tackle him myself, but before I had gone a yard – and I'll stand by this to my dying day! – the figure glided right through the brick wall.'

WALES

Clwyd

THE BLUE LION
(Cwm. Map reference: 26)

Geoffrey Copeland has a problem. He stoutly declares, 'I do not believe in the supernatural!' – yet he is the landlord of one of the most famous haunted pubs in Wales, and on top of that he has witnessed a couple of manifestations for which he can find no logical answer. He makes a point of the fact that he was sober on both occasions.

'Eight years ago I saw an ashtray literally float along the bar,' he told me. 'My wife caught it and put it back – and it disappeared along the bar again. I might add there was no water on the bar and no hover principle involved.

'Even more mystifying was something which happened after we had alterations carried out on the inn. One of the electric lamps attached to the old part of the building didn't light up on the opening day. I said, "Leave it, we'll fix it in a couple of days." But on the second day of the opening there was a power strike and the national grid went off. The whole of Cwm was blacked out, and there was no way for power to get through a circuit when that switch had been thrown. Yet the lamp which had not been working before came on!

'I just could not believe it. The following morning the electrician who had been working on the inn said, "Come on, we'll sort this out." We lifted the floorboards and found the two wires leading to the lamp were just lying on the bare earth – they had not even been connected up.

'There is no mechanical, physical or electrical way it could have happened. But, of course, when the grid came on again, that lamp went off.'

In his book *Ghosts of Wales* Peter Underwood, the president of the Ghost Club, described an equally strange phenomenon at the Blue Lion in the time of the previous landlord Stan Hughes. He installed a tiny zoo in an outbuilding at the back of the pub and his collection included two monkeys, three snakes and an alligator as well as a number of less spectacular pets. The animals lived in secure cages and to keep the place fresh and easy to clean sand was sprinkled over the floor.

What alarmed Mr Hughes was that frequently when he went into the animals' building he found the cages unlocked and the animals running about free. At first he thought a practical joker might be to blame so he carefully smoothed the sand over the floor to see if footprints would be left on it. But when he went to look on the following morning all he could see was the pawprints of his animals. Next he wound heavy wire round the locks of the cages but this made no difference. When he went to inspect the animals he found that the wire had been untwisted and they were loose again.

The ghost which traditionally haunts the Blue Lion is of a man called John Henry who was believed to have been murdered in the middle of the 17th century. Both Mr Hughes and his wife saw his apparition which has been described as wearing working clothes and with his trousers tied with thongs below the knees. In John Henry's day the pub building was a farmhouse in which a farmer lived with his two adult sons. It appears to have been a very quarrelsome family, and on one occasion the altercation between John on the one hand and his father and brother on the other grew so loud that neighbours called in the beadle. This dignitary managed to restore order, and a couple of days later he called back to make sure the peace was undisturbed. He was told by the father that John Henry had decided to leave home and had set off to find work abroad.

Nothing more was thought about the matter and as time passed John Henry was almost forgotten – until the turn of the century when an addition was made to the local church which meant moving some coffins from their resting places to new graves. When the sexton dug down to one coffin he was startled to find a man's skeleton sprawled on top of it. The disappearance of John Henry was recalled and it became the view of the locals that he had been killed at the farm during another family row, and his father and brother had disposed of his body by burying it in the churchyard.

THE TALACRE ARMS
(*Holywell. Map reference: 155*)

The poltergeist style haunting of the Talacre Arms began when landlord Mark Sumner had an old stable demolished in order to extend the pub's car park. Supernatural disapproval at the work was spectacular – glowing electric light bulbs plummeted from their sockets *and were only extinguished when they smashed on the floor*, and unseen hands pulled pints of mild. Three customers swore that they saw the pub piano playing by itself.

The effect of the haunting on the three dogs the landlord had in succession was tragic. The first ran away and was never heard of again. The second animal broke through a glass door panel when something sent it berserk, and afterwards was in such a state of tension that a new home had to be found for him, and the last dog raced out of the pub in a blind panic one night and was hit by a car.

'So many things have happened and so many people have witnessed them that I can't ignore them any longer,' Mr Sumner told the press in December 1979, and he went on to describe how he was once called from the kitchen to the bar by a dozen of his regulars who pointed excitedly to a picture.

'It was gently swinging to and fro suspended by one screw in the corner,' he said. 'Before, it had been securely fixed to the wall. Nobody could explain that.'

Although he believes it was the demolition of the stable which triggered off the activity he experienced, Mr Sumner added, 'I've met the previous owners and they verify that strange things happened before. They didn't tell me at the time because they thought I might not buy the place.'

Dyfed

THE CASTLE HOTEL
(Little Haven. Map reference: 35)

Probably the most supernaturally charged pub in Wales, the Castle Hotel has a fascinating variety of ghosts ancient and modern. Its best known and most traditional phantom is the White Lady who goes back to the 18th century when the Castle was a farmhouse. During that period a woman owned it who suffered a mysterious death, her body being found washed up on the beach with head wounds. It is not known whether or not she was a murder victim, but it was her glimmering figure glimpsed on the premises which began the house's reputation for being haunted.

Another ghost from two centuries ago is that of a hunchback, though like so many other phantoms it is not clear why he remains earthbound.

From Susan Nelson-Edwards, the wife of the landlord, I learned of the modern paranormal activity which centres on the hotel.

'Even when I am by myself here I never feel that I am alone,' she said. 'I always have the sensation of being watched. There is nothing nasty about it, one gets used to it just as one does to the sounds one sometimes hears.'

She explained this was like someone talking in a voice just low enough for it to be impossible to distinguish the actual words. Sometimes the phenomenon made her believe that the television set had been left on in the next room but when she went to switch it off she found that in fact it had been turned off. Mrs Nelson-Edwards added that the ghostly talking was accompanied by the rattle of a poker and fireirons. Perhaps it is a recurring echo from a fireside chat long ago – when one looks into a number of hauntings one soon realises that there is no rhyme or reason as to why certain happenings continue to be repeated down the ages. What we regard as significant does not seem to apply in the paranormal world.

'I am not the only one who has experienced odd happenings here,' Mrs Nelson-Edwards continued. 'Several people have experienced our invisible cat which jumps on their beds during the night. It feels like a perfectly ordinary cat landing on your counterpane, until you put your hand out and find there is nothing there.

'One Christmas not long ago my mother had an alarming experience at night when she went down into the bar to get some pop for the children. She was looking down at the floor when she saw two feet begin to materialise, and looking up she saw that a dark heavy-set man had appeared in front of her. Needless to say, she fled.

'My own sighting was equally mysterious because I was never able to find any explanation for it. I was at the foot of the stairs and when I looked up I saw a stranger at the top. He was tall and thin and wearing a very light brown suit. I remember an odd thing was that his features appeared hazy, but I would not have realised he was a ghost if he had not faded away in front of my eyes.'

THE KING'S HEAD HOTEL
(Llandeilo. Map reference: 93)

In 1982 an intriguing report on the King's Head appeared in the *News of the World*, telling how Gwendoline Lloyd had an extraordinary sensation when she entered the premises for the first time.

'I feel I was murdered here,' Mrs Lloyd announced to the surprised owner, David Legg. 'I was pushed out of a window overlooking a river.'

Later she told the newspaper, 'I knew nothing of the ghost when I walked into the pub for the first time. I just felt I was the reincarnation of a girl who had died there.'

'We have two ghosts here which various people have seen from time to time,' Mr Legg told me. 'They don't make noises or throw things about – they just make appearances. One is rarely seen. The other is the wife of a previous owner who wears a long white dress and has long auburn hair. It was always thought that she committed suicide by jumping from a window, but we now know she was murdered by being pushed out.'

Gwent

THE KING'S ARMS
(Abergavenny. Map reference: 89)

An elderly lady in old fashioned clothes, believed to have been the aunt of a brewer connected with the pub, is the phantom who has been glimpsed at the King's Arms.

In describing the apparition Sybil Gibbons, the wife of a previous landlord, said, 'An old woman came down the stairs and went through the lounge. She was wearing a long black skirt and a lace blouse.'

The brewer's aunt is blamed for nocturnal sounds and curious incidents on the premises.

'We had a picture on the wall in the bedroom,' John Gibbons said. 'It was regularly taken off the wall and put on the floor. When we finally moved it downstairs, it was never touched again.' Mr Gibbons believes that there is a second ghost at the pub which he described as 'a young girl who was ravished by a priest and died in childbirth'.

THE QUEEN'S HOTEL
(Monmouth. Map reference: 129)

This Tudor-style building has long had the reputation for being haunted by a Parliamentarian soldier from the time of the Civil War but, according to the landlord Mr Statham, his spectre has not been seen recently.

'Oliver Cromwell stayed at the inn during one of his campaigns,' he said. 'While he was here one of his soldiers named Jenkins tried to assassinate him, but the bodyguard shot and killed him. There are still a couple of musket ball holes in one of the A-frames of the building from that happening.'

The shadowy figure of Jenkins used to be seen in the

bedroom which was used by Cromwell, perhaps pondering on how different history would have been had his attempt succeeded.

THE SKIRRID MOUNTAIN INN
(Llanvihangel Crucorney. Map reference: 149)

No pub in the British Isles has such a tragic historical background as this inn, which claims to be the oldest in Wales, and at least one manifestation has reflected this dramatically. It happened when a lady sitting in the taproom with a friend suddenly felt faint. Her friend took her out hurriedly and then returned and asked for help because the lady had been taken ill. Landlord David Foster hurried to her with a glass of brandy and found that she was choking.

After she had been attended to and taken home, she told her family that it had felt as though she had a noose round her neck. Her son-in-law later told Mr Foster that the marks of a rope had actually appeared on her neck.

In explaining the significance of this, the landlord told me, 'The inn used to be used as a courthouse, quarterly assize courts being held on the top floor. The room now used as the upstairs bathroom was the condemned cell and those sentenced to death were hanged immediately in the stairway. There are records of 182 people being hanged there.

'While the court was in session the bottom part was still used as an inn. The farmers would be drinking down here while a prisoner was tried, and when he had been executed they would come out to inspect the body, which had been laid out on a slab, to be sure that they had hanged the right man.'

Apart from the incident related to what are known locally as 'the hanging stairs', the Skirrid Mountain Inn possesses a military phantom.

'My son-in-law woke up in one of the bedrooms and saw what he took to be a Cromwellian soldier standing at the window,' said Mr Foster. 'He was looking out towards the hills, and he had a cloak and the kind of helmet Parliamentary soldiers used to wear. My son-in-law was so frightened he tried to rouse my daughter but he was unable to speak. And then the apparition quietly disappeared.'

Some months later Mr Foster learned that the inn had once been used as a barracks by a troop of Cromwell's cavalry.

Gwynedd

THE BRIGANDS' INN
(Mallwyd. Map reference: 29)

This pub got its unusual name because over three centuries ago it really was a haunt of brigands – and since then one of the brigands has continued to haunt it. The odd thing about this phantom is that he is red-haired, like the rest of his fellow robbers who made up the dreaded *Twylliaid Cochich* – Welsh for 'the red-headed brigands'.

'The inn was the meeting place of the brigands of Mallwyd at the beginning of the 17th century,' said landlord Peter Huntingdon. 'All were red haired because of their Celtic origin. They had complete control of the district and no one could freely pass through the valley unless they were with an armed escort.

'In the end Baron Lewis Owen received a royal commission to wipe them out and he turned up at Christmas 1610, and immediately hanged eighty of them close to the inn. A year later a coach carrying the baron and the Earl of Caernarvon was ambushed and both men were murdered on the road in front of the inn.'

Mr Huntingdon said that he personally had not seen the Brigands' traditional ghost but he was reputed to haunt the old part of the pub.

Mid Glamorgan

THE BEECH TREE
(Ystrad Mynach. Map reference: 12)

Bob Smith is the name of the ghost who has frequently returned to The Beech Tree. In life he was an old man who lived in the workhouse opposite the pub at the beginning of this century.

'I was in the office one night and I saw somebody go past quickly,' said Margaret Bates who runs the pub with her husband Gerald. 'All I noticed was that it was a short person and I thought it was the cleaner but she had gone home. I saw him later . . . The cleaner has seen him, too, and the description fits Bob Smith.'

Mrs Bates' sighting of the ghost was shortly after she and her husband had moved into The Beech Tree, a circumstance which seems often to trigger an increase in paranormal activity in pubs. Perhaps the spectre of the old man who crossed the road from the workhouse for his regular pint was anxious to see the newcomers to his local.

THE CASTLE
(Maesteg. Map reference: 33)

'I was alone when I heard somebody walking around whistling a cheerful tune, but when I called out, nobody answered,' Malcolm Jones, landlord of The Castle, told the press in 1981. 'There was nobody there and the doors were all locked from the inside.'

The resident ghost responsible for odd happenings is believed to go back to the early 19th century when a landlord at the pub discovered that his wife was having an affair with the groom. Finding the man in the master bedroom – now Room No 5 – he killed him in a fit of rage and then hid the body beneath the floorboards. But the crime did not remain secret for long. The disappearance of the groom, coupled with rumours of his liaison with the publican's wife, caused the premises to be searched. When the murderer learned that the floorboards in his room had been raised he hanged himself.

Today guests who stay in Room No 5 frequently complain of drops in the temperature.

'One guest was terribly afraid,' Gloria Jones, the wife of the landlord, was reported as saying. 'He slept with the lights on and the door and window open. We had to give him another room.'

A member of the staff saw a phantom lady, and there is speculation as to whether she could have been the landlord's wife whose infidelity led to the murder.

'The barman was locking up when he saw a woman going into the Ladies,' said Malcolm Jones. 'When she didn't come out, he knocked on the door. There was no answer. He broke open the door, and the loo was empty.'

THE HIGH CORNER
(Llanharan. Map reference: 82)

A ghost with poltergeist-like tendencies haunts The High Corner in a way that is traditional in a number of pubs with supernatural reputations. Here objects vanish and reappear in places where they would not have remained concealed.

'A gift from my mother completely disappeared,' said landlady Mickey Barker. 'Two years later when my mother died, it fell out of a cupboard. The cupboard was used regularly, so it wouldn't have just gone unnoticed.' She also described how on one occasion the lamps in the bar began swinging on their own accord and two customers had a lucky escape when a crest which was hung above the bar crashed between them.

The ghost itself has been seen by a member of the staff who said, 'I saw a man standing in front of the dining-room fireplace. I went cold when I saw him. He had black hair and wore black clothes.' It was realised he was a phantom when he faded away.

THE PRINCE OF WALES
(Kenfig Hill. Map reference: 125)

Ghostly organ music is the phenomenon experienced by landlord Michael Evans late at night in this six-centuries-old pub.

'It's a funny old place and serves a very scattered community,' he said. 'Apart from being a pub it is used for meetings of the town council, as a polling station and a chapel.'

The room used by chapel folk is upstairs and on three occasions when the pub had been locked up for the night Mr Evans heard the sound of the organ coming sonorously down the stairs leading to it.

'We thought that some kids or vandals had broken in and were playing about with the organ in the chapel room,' Mr Evans explained. 'I took the two dogs with me and went to investigate, but the dogs would go no further than halfway up the stairs. I went on alone and as I opened the door of the room the music stopped. It was all in darkness.'

The Prince of Wales recently became news around the world due to more remarkable – and non-supernatural – sounds from the past. The experiments, which are still being conducted there as I write, may ultimately shed light on what we now regard as paranormal phenomena.

Mr Evans told me, 'Two of my regulars – one an industrial chemist and one an electrical engineer – read an article in the national press about some experiments being done in Germany in a building constructed of materials containing silica which is found in sandstone and other rocks. The object of the experiments was to try and amplify sounds which in the past had been "recorded" on the silica over the years.

'These two chaps decided to try the same thing here. They concocted some electronic gear and began their experiments. They have recorded some remarkable sounds which included organ music, choral singing, voices, footsteps and the ticking of a clock – and we haven't got a clock with a loud tick.'

SCOTLAND

Dumfries and Galloway

THE COUNTY HOTEL
(Dumfries. Map reference: 43)

The County's reputation as Scotland's most famous haunted hotel is not based on spectacular paranormal phenomena but because of the exalted position its ghost holds in the history and hearts of Scotland. The resident phantom is Bonnie Prince Charlie who, according to the Scottish Tourist Board, 'constantly wore a frustrated look and appeared so often that a lounge was named after him'.

On 23 July, 1745, Charles Edward – known affectionately as the 'Young Chevalier' or 'Bonnie Prince Charlie' – landed with seven followers at Eriskay in the Hebrides in an attempt to win the kingdom his father, the Old Pretender, had failed to gain in the Jacobite Rebellion of 1715. By 17 September Edinburgh had surrendered to Charles Edward's Highland army and he symbolically held court at Holyrood Palace in the tradition of his ancestors. Four days later the rebels defeated a royal army under the command of Sir John Cope.

The way south was now clear and on 1 November the prince started out for London with an army of 6,500. He managed to get as far as Derby and alarm spread through London as England's best regiments were fighting on the Continent, and plans were drawn up to evacuate the royal family to Hanover. But the Jacobite tide turned at Derby when the prince's bickering commanders persuaded him to return to Scotland where, at Falkirk, the rebels won their last victory over an army loyal to George II. On 16 April, 1746, the hopes of the Jacobites were dashed forever at Drummossie Moor, now known as Culloden.

In the closing weeks of the rebellion the prince stayed at the Commercial Inn – which later became the County Hotel – in Dumfries where the townsfolk raised the then tremendous sum of two thousand pounds for the Jacobite cause.

Since the terrible days which followed the Scots' defeat, the phantom of the prince returns not to Culloden Moor, as do the spectres of some of his followers, but to the County Hotel. The apparition was first in the news in 1936 when a hotel guest in the lounge named after the prince beheld a figure, said to be dressed like a Jacobite, appear from a closet doorway and stand on the Royal Stewart tartan carpet with an expression of deep and anxious thought, as indeed the prince must have done 190 years earlier.

After a few moments the figure turned and went back through the same door. Later the guest learned two things which caused him no little surprise – that the door through which the spectre appeared was traditionally kept sealed, and that the room behind it was the one which Bonnie Prince Charlie had slept in.

Following that there have been other appearances of the anxious prince but the door has remained locked. Recently viewers of Border Television saw the haunted hotel on their screens and heard the story of the haunting from Border's 'Look Around' presenter Eric Wallace. At one point Eric was seen to come through the door like the royal ghost but this was due to what he called the 'magic of television' rather than any other agency – and the door is still never opened.

THE KING'S ARMS HOTEL
(Dumfries. Map reference: 43)

According to the Scottish Tourist Board the King's Arms was haunted by a young woman in her early twenties who has been reported enthusiastically in the Scottish press on several occasions. She haunted the hotel for over a hundred years, and when she has been seen she was described as being dressed in Victorian clothes. Why she lingered at the King's Arms is not known, but it seems that she has an interest in the modern world – she is said to have enjoyed watching television in the lounge.

THE OLD SMUGGLERS INN
(Auchencairn. Map reference: 114)

After a programme by Border Television on the Old Smugglers Inn it became a Mecca for those interested in the supernatural. This was curiously appropriate because the resident ghost – known as Gladys at the pub – appears to have an obsession with electronic equipment and electricity.

'There have been a number of mysterious happenings – electrical things being switched on and switched off,' the landlord's mother-in-law told me. 'The ghost seems to be addicted to electricity, and we can only think that she was some previous owner who is fascinated by it since she came back. A typical example was a music centre which switched itself on full blast at half past two in the morning, though we know for a fact it was off when we went to bed.'

Apart from such tricks which include the turning on and off of the pub lights, Gladys makes her presence known by footfalls in an empty attic. Also associated with her is a cold zone at one end of the house where customers shiver when they walk into it. Occasionally the phantom has been glimpsed.

'Last year I was sitting up in bed reading when I saw a shadow moving across the room,' the mother of the landlord's wife said. 'I'm not fanciful, but there is no doubt I saw it. It was just as though a shadow had gone across the light. I got down under the covers and that was the end of my reading for the night.'

Fife

FERNIE CASTLE HOTEL
(Ladybank. Map reference: 62)

One of the most popular hotels among ghost-hunters is the Fernie Castle, despite the fact that the landlord says that he has not seen anything of a paranormal nature himself. Visitors from the United States in particular are fascinated by the legend of the Green Lady who in the past has been seen in the vicinity of the old castle hotel's tower.

'It seems that during the persecution of the Protestants by the Catholics the young owner of the house, the Laird of Fernie, was murdered and his wife threw herself out of a window,' the present landlord told me. 'Now she is supposed to haunt the tower wearing a long green floating dress.'

Highlands

THE KYLESKU HOTEL
(Kylesku. Map reference: 94)

The Kylesku Hotel, which stands at the head of Loch Cairnbawn on the remote north-west coast, used to be the old ferry house, and it is agreed that the phantom which appears under a trapdoor leading to the loft returns from that time. However, there are conflicting views as to whose ghost it is.

One tradition goes back to the 1890s when the landlady of the ferry house was a Miss MacKay who was famous locally as a fiddler. It is said that she often played while her brother served the drinks and the inn became very popular. And perhaps she was not too strict as a publican, because a policeman tricked her into losing her licence so that she and her brother had to leave to the deep regret of the local people. And the ghost? Some say that it is the shade of Miss MacKay's brother who refuses to quit the place which he enjoyed so much.

The alternative tradition is much more tragic. It tells that the Kylesku ghost is that of an old fisherman who was nicknamed Tordeas. One day he was walking along the shore of Kerrachar Bay when his eyes lighted on a keg which had been washed up by the tide. When he pulled out the bung he found that it was full of whisky.

Hardly able to credit his good fortune, the old man carried it back to the ferry house. Not wishing to drink alone, he invited his son and some friends to share in his windfall, and they took the keg up a ladder into the loft to have an undisturbed carousal.

The men had never enjoyed such a plentiful supply of free liquor before and soon all were rolling drunk. At this point a quarrel broke out between Tordeas and his son on some family question. Tempers inflamed by the whisky rose out of all proportion to the matter, and before long father and son were grappling together. The young man forced Tordeas backwards and suddenly he vanished – he had stepped back through the loft's open trapdoor.

On the floor below he died of a broken neck, using his last breaths to promise that he would return for his revenge. A few months later the son was drowned, and it is claimed that Tordeas' ghost still appears at midnight on the anniversary of the patricide.

Lanarkshire

THE APPLEBANK INN
(Larkhall. Map reference: 7)

A spectre in a sari is an unlikely apparition for a Scottish pub, yet the ghost of the Applebank Inn was an Indian princess in life.

'Several of my customers claim to have seen her or been aware of her presence,' said William Foy, owner of the Applebank Inn. 'She goes back to when Captain McNeil, a local laird, returned home bringing an Indian wife with him. He set up house, but after some time his wife disappeared under very mysterious circumstances.'

It would seem that the unfortunate lady – regarded as a 'heathen' in those days – was rejected by the local gentry, and as a result she lost the affection of her husband. Later the McNeil residence was destroyed by fire.

'A stone lintel, bearing the McNeil motif, was transferred from the ruined house to this pub which stood in the captain's grounds,' Mr Foy said. 'The Black Lady's visitations are believed to have some association with the lintel which is still here.'

It would seem that a certain amount of poltergeist activity is connected with the haunting. There have been reports of glasses being flung off the bar by an invisible force, beer bottles suddenly bursting of their own accord, and a strange night when fishermen on the nearby River Avon heard weird noises issuing from the inn when it was closed.

Strathclyde

THE SHIELDHILL HOUSE HOTEL
(Quothquan. Map reference: 147)

'Who's that lady on the stairs, Mummy?' the little girl asked, pointing at the hotel staircase. Her mother did not tell her it was rude to point, she was too surprised at her daughter's question when she could see clearly that there was no one there. Yet the six-year-old was so adamant that she had seen a lady in a grey dress that her mother questioned her closely and realised that her daughter was describing the Grey Lady who is the traditional ghost of the hotel.

'The story goes back to the middle of the last century,' Mrs Hennah of the Shieldhill House Hotel told me. 'Then a wealthy farmer lived here who became enraged when he discovered that his daughter had a liaison with a local lad of humble origins. In order to prevent her going out to meet him he locked the girl in an upstairs room.

'Determined to keep an assignation with her lover, the girl attempted to climb down from her window by means of the ivy growing on the wall. Unfortunately it was not strong enough to bear her weight, and she fell to her death.'

Down the road from the hotel there is a burial ground attached to a now deserted church, and here a headstone bears out the tragic story.

NORTHERN IRELAND

Antrim (Ulster)

DOBBIN'S INN HOTEL
(Carrickfergus. Map reference: 56)

Carrickfergus boasts one of the best preserved castles in Ireland, and one of the things which intrigue the tourists who visit is the story of a secret escape passage leading to Dobbin's Inn Hotel. This tunnel is haunted by the inn's ghost who is known to the staff as Maude.

'The inn was once a tower house – a type of small castle in medieval times – part of which has been replaced with a modern building,' I was told by Rosemary Strange, one of the hotel proprietors. 'A long time ago it was owned by Sheriff Dobbin of County Fergus and we believe that the ghost was his daughter. The legend goes that she was an unfaithful wife and on one occasion her husband found out that she had a boyfriend up in her room. He drew his sword and ran up the stairs to kill his rival, but he met her coming down the stairs and she accidentally ran on to his sword and was killed.

'We have some secret passages here and she wanders along them, and she makes her presence felt in the hotel as well.

'A lot of people – especially before we took over the place five years ago – have seen her. And there are unbelievable tales of long-term residents here who built up relationships with the ghost who appeared quite frequently.

'On one occasion a lady who had second sight was in the coffee lounge talking to one of the owners and she said suddenly, "I feel the presence of a young girl but she is not a harmful spirit." '

Apparently before Maude materialises the temperature plunges, and in the past members of the staff who have stayed up in the hope of seeing her reported a feeling of intense cold before she appeared. Another aspect of the haunting is the flinging of cups and glasses off shelves by an unseen force.

'Sometimes the internal phones used to ring mysteriously,' said Rosemary Strange. 'It happened to me, and I found there was no one in the rooms to have used them. The phones just rang by themselves. It happened quite a lot when there were functions. It seems that she did not approve of alcohol.'

If this is so the ghost must be upset once a year when a medieval banquet is held at Carrickfergus Castle. Guests wear medieval dress and meet at Dobbin's Inn for a traditional quaffing of mead before going to the castle in procession.

EIRE

THE BLACK CHAPEL INN
(Rathcoole. Map reference: 20)

The entity which haunted the Black Chapel Inn – which stands on the site of an ancient hospice – is unique in the annals of ghostlore. In haunted pubs one expects phantoms and mysterious sounds and poltergeists who play mischievous tricks on staff and customers, but only this pub can boast a haunted glove.

Its first owner was the notorious Lady Mornington, an erstwhile friend of the Duke of Wellington, who left behind a glove after an escapade at the inn. According to tradition the glove remained lost for sixty years, and when it was found the landlord and staff were surprised by its pristine condition. No dust or cobwebs adhered to it – it might have been cast aside by her ladyship a few minutes earlier. But this was only the first curious aspect of the Mornington glove.

In order to preserve this memento of titled patronage, the landlord had a special glass case constructed to house it, and thus it was exhibited in the bar. Before long the regulars were paying the glass case a lot of attention – something strange had happened inside it. When it had first been placed in the glass-sided box, the glove lay limp on the bottom but before long it had filled out to give the impression of being worn by an invisible hand.

From then on Lady Mornington's glove developed a life of its own. To the mystification of all at the Black Chapel the sealed case would be sometimes found empty when members of the staff opened up in the morning. But the glove – which has been the inspiration of at least one famous horror story – would be lying on the bar with its fingers extended. What is not known is whether it was the glove itself which had been invested with some supernatural power, or whether the motivating force was the invisible hand of Lady Mornington.

KYTELER'S INN
(Kilkenny. Map reference: 95)

There is a tradition in Kilkenny that for six centuries the

building known as Kyteler's Inn has been haunted by the ghost of a witch. It began as an inn and in the last couple of years it has become one again after a period of being put to other uses. It is ideal for the purpose; the garden at its rear runs pleasantly down to the River Nore, it has a picturesque enclosed courtyard and the unusual feature of two wells in its grounds – above all it has one of the most remarkable backgrounds that it is possible for a pub to have.

'Now Kyteler's Inn has reverted to its old use,' Ned Comerford, one of the new owners told me. 'It is such a place as William Hazlitt would have loved to take his ease. As far as the ghost is concerned I have not experienced anything abnormal in the two years I have been at the inn, but I do know of people who have lived here who have sworn the place is haunted. The ghost is supposed to be of a woman named Petronilla who, in 1324, became the first woman in Ireland to be burned for witchcraft.'

The events which led up to her execution involved one of the most colourful female characters in Irish history – Dame Alice le Kyteler, who, if she had not escaped mysteriously to England, probably would have also haunted the inn which bears her name.

Dame Alice was born in 1280, the daughter of a Norman banker, a word which in those days meant a moneylender – an unpopular occupation which she carried on as a family business. Her first husband was William Outlawe, and after his death she married three husbands in quick succession, which kept the tongues of local gossips wagging. According to some notes published on the inn: 'Alice prospered in business and while she seems to have had an unusual flair for moneymaking she must also have been a person of outstanding beauty, or she could not have been as attractive as she was to so many men, nor would men have lavished wealth on her unless she was something of a siren . . .'

It is believed that she used her charms to attract bored husbands to her hostelry – Ned Comerford said there is a strong suspicion that she ran a brothel at Kyteler's Inn. And worse suspicions were aroused when she was noticed sweeping the dust of Kilkenny Street towards her door (in itself an occupation far beneath her) muttering the couplet:

'To the house of William my sonne,
hie all the wealth of Kilkennie towne.'

Rumours spread that she had got rid of her late husbands by magical means, that she was a witch and her great wealth resulted from an unholy alliance with an evil spirit who sometimes appeared in the form of a black dog. It was whispered that she called him 'Art Artisson', placated him with animal sacrifices, and that he was her demonic paramour. It was also said that she had in her house a number of comely young women to whom she taught magical arts, and who were the bait to lure men to her abode. Her chief confidante and helper in these affairs was a woman from Meath named Petronilla.

Finally the stories reached the ears of the Lord Bishop of Ossory, Richard de Ledrede, who made a formal complaint against her to the Chancellor of Ireland, demanding the immediate arrest of her, her coven and her many associates. Unfortunately for the bishop Alice's friends were rich and powerful and, when he resisted the request that he should withdraw the charges, they were able to have him arrested and imprisoned in Kilkenny.

But any satisfaction Dame Alice may have had from the humbling of her enemy did not last long. After seventeen days the bishop secured his release with the result that the Lord Justiciar of Ireland, Johan d'Arcy, took the unusual step of going to Kilkenny to try Dame Alice himself. Following his examination she was 'by common consent of all the judges secular and religious pronounced guilty of sorcery and magic, of heresy and of having sacrificed to demons, and she was ordered to be handed over to the secular authority to be duly punished'.

This meant that she, Petronilla and her young women were to be whipped through the streets at the cart's tail and then burned alive. But some of Dame Alice's friends remained loyal, and her escape was arranged the night before the execution. According to a contemporary Narrative she was 'supported by certaine of the nobilitie, and hastlie conveied over into England since which time it could never be understood what became of her'.

Her accomplices were not so lucky. Before being whipped

and burned, Petronilla confessed that, urged on by Dame Alice, she had renounced Christ, had sacrificed to demons and had brewed concoctions to afflict the bodies of Christians, and had practised other abominations. She added that her own magical powers were not as strong as those of her mistress who had instructed her in all these things, and much more besides.

According to the Narrative the bishop ordered that a huge fire should be lit in the centre of the city into which was thrown a sack of witch ointments which Dame Alice used 'to perpetrate her sorceries'. At another fire before the Tholsel – and watched by a vast crowd of people – Petronilla and Dame Alice's 'young ladies' were burned at the stake. Thus died, concluded the Narrative, 'the first heretical witch amongst so many so great who have ever been burned in Ireland'.

THE LEINSTER LODGE
(Kildare Town. Map reference: 99)

The haunting of the Leinster Lodge can only be described as bizarre – I am sure that only in Ireland could one find a talking boiler! The story goes back to the last decade of the 19th century when the then landlord died suddenly. The next morning a member of the staff, whose duties took him down into the cellar, was aghast to hear strange noises booming out of the boiler.

When the man told his story to the new owner, he was told that the death of his previous employer was no excuse to get drunk to the stage of hearing an inanimate object like a boiler conversing with him. Furthermore, if he did not go down to the cellar and stoke it up right away, his future at the pub would be in considerable doubt.

Grumbling, the man went down the cellar steps but a few minutes later he reappeared white-faced. Once more he had heard a grumble of voices echoing from it. The owner decided to investigate and when he too was subjected to the aural phenomenon, he gave orders for the boiler to be dismantled and taken away to the scrapyard.

When the work began the cellar was filled with strange and terrifying sounds and the men hastily dropped their tools. To everyone's relief the owner had a wall constructed to seal off the vociferous appliance – and so it has remained. It is an interesting question as to whether it would become vocal again if it was restored and brought into use.

THE PORTLAW INN
(Portlaw. Map reference: 124)

A popular theme in Victorian melodrama was the return of a victim's ghost to haunt its murderer or to apprise the living of its tragic fate. The latter circumstance happened at the Portlaw Inn when a young man connected with the establishment returned there as a phantom after he had been brutally murdered nearby.

According to the local tradition this occurred last century. The landlady of the inn had been puzzled by the non-appearance of the young man, and when she looked up from her work one morning and saw him in the bar she was about to ask where he had been. But the words died in her throat when she looked closer. His features were unnaturally white and there was a mistiness about the body which immediately told the woman that she was in the presence of a spectre.

With a slow, sad gesture the young man beckoned to her and turned to the door. It is well known that Irish landladies are made of stern stuff, and this one was no exception. While lesser mortals might have fainted, or at least reached for the brandy, she pulled her shawl round her shoulders and followed the apparition.

The slightly luminous figure led her along a path through some fields to a lonely spot where he had been waylaid the night before. Here it paused and pointed to the ground, then faded away. The landlady looked at the spot and saw the young man's huddled corpse lying there and soon afterwards she took the police to the scene of the murder.

Turpin Pubs

THE BELL
(Stilton, Cambridgeshire. Map reference: 13)

THE CHEQUERS
(Bickley, Kent. Map reference: 39)

THE GEORGE
(Buckden, Cambridgeshire. Map reference: 67)

THE GEORGE
(Wallingford, Oxfordshire. Map reference: 70)

THE OLDE BLACK BEAR
(Tewkesbury, Gloucestershire. Map reference: 117)

THE SPANIARDS
(Hampstead, London. Map reference: 8)

If Dick Turpin's ghost visits all the scenes it is supposed to haunt, the phantom of Black Bess must have her work cut out keeping up with the schedule. Being England's most famous highwayman, it is understandable that a number of old inns claim to have been used by Turpin, and a few are said to be haunted by manifestations of him.

Glamorous legends have grown up around him and he has frequently been referred to as a 'gentleman of the road', yet investigation of his career reveals nothing gentlemanly about him. The truth is that he was a vicious criminal.

The son of a tavern-keeper, he was born in 1705 in the Essex town of Hempstead. As he grew up he was apprenticed to a Whitechapel butcher, and when he had qualified at his trade he married the daughter of another tavern-keeper and opened his own business. All went well until farmers in the neighbourhood began missing livestock. They formed a vigilante committee and finally tracked their stolen beasts to Turpin's shop. Before they could catch him he fled from the district.

Having become used to money jingling in his pockets, the young man joined up with the infamous Essex Gang. This band was probably the most notorious collection of ruffians to terrorise folk in the 18th century. They specialised in robbing elderly farmers in remote farmhouses.

A typical example of how they operated occurred in Loughton where they broke into the home of an aged widow. At first she defied them, refusing to reveal where her money was hidden, but when Turpin said, 'If you don't tell us, I'll hold you over the fire!' her courage faltered and she pointed to the hiding place. The gang got away with her life's savings of £100.

The public outcry against the gang became so great that the authorities, backed by the militia, were forced to hunt them down. In the end most of its members were taken to Tyburn Tree, the place of public execution where Marble Arch now stands.

Among those who managed to escape the net was Dick Turpin. He teamed up with Tom King who, in 1736, was given the punning title of 'King of the Highwaymen'. Turpin introduced Tom to his secret hideout which was a cave in the heart of Epping Forest. Camouflaged by undergrowth, it was large enough to conceal their horses, yet close enough to the highway to allow them to make hold-ups and then vanish before the hue and cry began. So successful was this partnership in robbing lonely travellers that soon a £100 reward was offered for King or Turpin. Their reign of terror ended in May 1737, when Turpin stole a splendid racehorse from a certain Mr Major. Furious at the loss, Mr Major had posters printed giving its description and offering a large reward for information concerning its whereabouts.

Soon afterwards he received information from the landlord of the Red Lion in Whitechapel that a horse with white legs, answering to the poster's description, had been left in his stables. Mr Major went to the Red Lion and identified the animal as his 'White Stockings'. He then arranged for some constables to be stationed close to the inn and when a man arrived to collect the horse he was immediately arrested. In order to lighten his sentence, he confessed that he was Tom King's brother who, he said, was in hiding at an inn at Goodman's Field.

Within hours an armed party arrived at the inn and broke into it, taking Tom King by surprise. Shots were exchanged, in the middle of which Turpin galloped up. He raised his pistol to shoot the landlord, whom he thought had betrayed them, but the ball struck King instead.

'My God, Dick, you have killed me!' moaned King as he collapsed. Turpin turned his horse and spurred to safety. From then on he continued his career alone, wanted for murder as well as robbery.

His notoriety spread from Epping to the dreaded Hounslow Heath where the bodies of executed road agents hung from gibbets in creaking chains. Perhaps it was the sight of the dangling corpses that caused Turpin to suddenly disappear – to the great relief of all travellers. But next year his name was news again due to an extraordinary coincidence.

In the Yorkshire town of Welton a prosperous stranger had set up business as a horse-dealer. He became popular in local taverns and was greatly admired for his marksmanship and skill as a rider. One evening he was sitting with some friends at his premises when a gamecock flew by. He raised his musket and shot the bird on the wing.

'Well done, Palmer!' applauded his companions, but the neighbour, to whom the bird belonged, was furious.

'That was a dishonest act, and it seems to me that dishonesty becomes you,' he cried.

The horse-dealer replied by pulling a pistol from the pocket of his greatcoat and shouting, 'Keep a civil tongue in your head or you will be as dead as your bird.'

The neighbour hastily removed himself and had the horse-dealer John Palmer arrested for threatening his life. The local magistrate made inquiries and a disturbing suggestion came to light that Palmer's premises were a clearing place for horses which had been stolen throughout the country. While further investigations were being made Palmer was imprisoned in a cell at York Castle, where he remained for several months.

In an endeavour to get his name cleared he wrote to his brother-in-law in London, begging him to come to York and prove his good character. Unfortunately for Palmer he forgot to pay the postage fee, with the result that his brother-in-law refused to pay for the letter and it was returned to the Post Office.

Here it was seen by a clerk named Smith who, earlier in life, had taught as a schoolmaster at Hempstead in Essex. As he looked at the returned envelope he recognised the handwriting of one of his old pupils – a certain Richard Turpin.

He immediately informed the authorities and was taken with other witnesses to York where Palmer was unmasked and, as Dick Turpin, condemned to death.

Thanks to Harrison Ainsworth's novel *Rookwood* Turpin has been credited with making a fantastic ride from London to York. In fact he never made it, it was the exploit of a lesser-known highwayman called John Nevison who rode from Gravesend to York on a bay mare in fifteen hours to establish an alibi after a robbery.

A pub which had a very strong reputation for being haunted by Turpin was The Bell Inn at Stilton. It was from this inn that the famous Stilton cheese used to be distributed, but when I visited the town James Barnes, who has been a resident of Stilton since 1926, told me that the Bell had closed its doors for the last time some years ago.

'It used to have a great copper sign weighing a quarter of a ton,' he recalled. 'That was stolen quite a long time ago. I remember people saying the inn was haunted by Dick Turpin.'

I learned that the ghostly highwayman revisited The Bell only on Wednesday nights. In the old days customers claimed the drumming hoofbeats of his horse were heard, and a few swore to having seen the shape of a rider bending low over his mount gallop up to the inn and vanish under the old archway. Perhaps the pair still re-enact this part of some forgotten journey.

It is believed that the phantom seen at The Chequers, in Bickley, was that of Dick Turpin. There is a local tradition that the highwayman used to frequent the inn, part of which goes back to the 16th century, and that on several occasions he made a hasty exit down the back stairs from the room where he used to sleep in a large four-poster. On one occasion a lady customer saw a man 'in fancy dress' seated in this room. She found the encounter alarming although she did not realise she had seen an apparition until she told the staff about the man in 18th century clothing of green velvet.

Apart from this elegant apparition, the pub has other supernatural manifestations such as a lady in an old fashioned dress seen gliding along the upstairs passage and the sound of footsteps echoing in empty rooms and on the stairs – perhaps the latter were an echo from one of Turpin's quick departures.

Another hotel with a Turpin-ghost tradition is The George at Buckden in Cambridgeshire. One of the rooms has been named after him, and there is a story that his phantom used to ride up to the inn though the details have become hazy with the passage of time.

The oldest inn in Gloucestershire is the Olde Black Bear which, along with its alarming phantom of a decapitated man dragging chains behind him, has a legend of a ghostly Dick Turpin who in life used to tie Black Bess to a tree close to the pub ready for a quick get-away.

The George at Wallingford – already mentioned in this book – had a trapdoor in a room above its archway which legend tells was installed for the use of Turpin should the officers of the law pay him a surprise visit when he stayed there, but the pub with the best known reputation as a haunt of the highwayman is The Spaniards at Hampstead in London. He used its cellars to hide from the law and after his execution landlords there heard the sound of Black Bess galloping over the heath. Today the inn displays several Turpin mementoes, including a pistol ball in a small glass case. A fading document explains that it was a ball fired by the highwayman at a royal mail coach.

The Blue Posts' Melodrama

Alas the old Blue Posts Inn is no more but the haunting associated with it had such a fine Dickensian flavour that I believe the story is still worth telling. It is recounted in the diary of the Reverend Richard Harris Barham, the author of *The Ingoldsby Legends*. It concerned friends of his, and he prefaced it by saying, 'It is one of the best authenticated ghost stories in existence.'

He learned of the bedroom drama from his friend Mrs Hastings after she and her husband, Captain Hastings R.N., had travelled to Portsmouth by coach. With them was a Mr Hamilton who had been appointed to the naval dockyard there. As the coach rolled into the town and passed one of its narrow lanes, Mrs Hastings asked Mr Hamilton why he had suddenly gone so grave and silent.

'It was the recollection of the lane we have just passed, and of a very singular circumstance which occurred at a house in it some eighteen years ago,' he said with a shiver. 'As we are old friends and I know you will not laugh at me, I will repeat it to you.'

Mr Hamilton went on to explain that eighteen years ago he arrived in Portsmouth to join a ship to 'proceed abroad on a mercantile speculation'. He found his ship had not yet docked, and as two or three naval ships had just been paid off in the harbour, coupled with a county election and the fact the town was filled with people waiting on an overdue outward bound fleet, all the inns in Portsmouth were full.

'After wandering half over the town without success, I at length happened to inquire at a tolerably decent-looking public house situated in the lane alluded to, where a very civil, though a very cross looking, landlady at length made me happy by the intelligence that she would take me in, if I did not mind sleeping in a double-bedded room,' Mr Hamilton said. 'I certainly did object to a fellow lodger, and so I told her, but, as I coupled the

238

objection with an offer to pay handsomely for both beds though I should occupy only one of them, a bargain was settled, and I took possession of my apartment.'

When Mr Hamilton retired for the night he looked at both beds and found one had a 'decent counterpane' while the other was covered with a coarse but clean patchwork quilt. He decided on the bed with the decent counterpane, put his portmanteau beside the bed and having carefully locked the door to keep out intruders, went to bed and fell asleep.

'I had slept I suppose an hour or more when I was awakened by a noise in the lane below,' he told his friends, 'but being convinced that it was merely occasioned by the breaking up of a jolly party, I was turning round to recompose myself, when I perceived, by the light of the moon which shone brightly into the room, that the bed opposite was occupied by a man, having the appearance of a sailor. He was only partially undressed, having his trousers on, and what appeared to be a belcher handkerchief, tied round his head by way of a nightcap. His position was half-sitting, half-reclining on the outside of the bed, and he seemed to be asleep.'

Mr Hamilton was naturally angry that the landlady should have broken the bargain when he had paid for both beds, and at first he thought he should make the other man quit the room. But he was a kindly man and as the stranger seemed quiet and asleep, he decided to let him rest, although he was determined to give the landlady a piece of his mind.

'It was broad daylight when I awoke in the morning,' Mr Hamilton continued, 'and the sun was shining full in through the window. My slumbering friend apparently had never moved, for there he was still, half-sitting, half-lying on the quilt, and I had a fair opportunity of observing his features, which were not ill-favoured, and were set off by a pair of bushy black whiskers that would have done honour to a rabbi. What surprised me most, however, was that I could now plainly perceive that what I had taken in the moonlight for a red handkerchief on his forehead was in reality a white one, but quite saturated in parts with a crimson fluid, which trickled down his left cheek, and seemed to run upon the pillow.'

Mr Hamilton was puzzled as to how the stranger could have entered the room when he had locked the door on the inside, especially as he was certain no one had been hiding in the room when he entered. He walked over to the door to inspect the lock and found it fastened with the key in place just as he had left it. He decided to cross the room to the occupied bed to get an explanation from the sailor, but, as he turned from the door, to his astonishment the stranger was nowhere to be seen.

Mr Hamilton then searched the room for some concealed exit, but could not find one. In a very puzzled mood, he dressed and went downstairs and sought out the landlady, demanding his bill and telling her he would not bother to breakfast after the breach of promise respecting the privacy of his room. At this her face flushed and she demanded what he meant.

'You asked for the whole room and you had the whole room,' she declared, 'and though I say it, there is not a more comfortable room in Portsmouth. I might have let the spare bed five times over, and refused to do so because you asked me.'

He stopped her tirade by putting a guinea on the bar, saying mildly that he did not wish to complain of any actual inconvenience from the presence of his fellow lodger, but because he had paid double he expected the conditions to be observed. However, he was now convinced the sharing of the room had happened without her consent and that some of her people had no doubt introduced the man to the room, not knowing of their understanding.

'What man?' demanded the landlady. 'There was no one in your room unless you let him in yourself. Had you not the key, and did not I hear you lock the door after you?'

Mr Hamilton replied this was true, but added, 'There certainly was a man – a sailor – in my room last night; though I know no more how he got in or out than I do where he got his broken head, or his unconscionable whiskers.' With these words he strode to the door of the inn, and then noticed the landlady had gone deathly pale.

'I hesitated, and at length a single word, uttered distinctly but lowly, and as if breathlessly spoken, fell upon my ear; it was "Whiskers!" "Yes, whiskers," I replied, "I never saw so splendid a pair in my life. And the broken . . .".'

'For heaven's sake come back one moment,' she gasped.

Mr Hamilton stepped back into the inn, surprised the word 'whiskers' should have such an effect on the woman. The landlady then begged him to tell her 'without disguise, who and what he saw in his bedroom last night'. He described the sailor, adding that he presumed he had taken refuge there from some drunken affray to sleep off the effects of his liquor, for although he had obviously been knocked about, he did not appear to be aware of his condition.

'Lord have mercy upon me!' the woman cried in terror. 'It's all true and the house is ruined forever!'

Then she told her alarmed guest that on the third evening before his arrival, a party of sailors from one of the ships were drinking at her inn when a quarrel broke out between them and some marines. Angry words soon led to blows.

'The landlady in vain endeavoured to interfere, till at length a heavy blow, struck with the edge of a pewter pot, lighting upon the temple of a stout young fellow of five and twenty, who was one of the most active on the side of the sailors, brought him to the ground, senseless and covered with blood,' continued Mr Hamilton. 'He never spoke again, but although his friends immediately conveyed him upstairs and placed him on the bed, endeavouring to staunch the blood and doing all in their power to save him, he breathed his last in a few minutes.'

In order to hush up the matter which would bring trouble to all concerned, the landlady agreed to the body being buried in the garden. The sailors and marines considered that, as he had just been paid off, no enquiry for him would take place.

'But it was all for no use,' cried the landlady, wringing her hands. 'I shall never dare to put anyone in your room again, for there it was he was carried, but they never could stop the bleeding till all was over. As sure as you are standing there a living man, he is come back to trouble us, for if he had been sitting to you for his picture, you could not have painted him more accurately than you have done.'

The Reverend Barham's story intrigued me so much that I made further inquiries and found that the inn concerned was known as the Blue Posts Inn, the original building of which was burned down in 1870. But, more than two centuries after the sailor had been killed, a final echo of the affair was reported in the *Star* newspaper on 21 February 1938.

Under the heading of MEMORY OF MURDER 200 YEARS AGO, a reporter told how a tombstone had been set up in the little courtyard where the sailor had been buried. The story concluded: 'To appease the ghost and to make up for his not being buried in consecrated ground, flowers were frequently placed on the spot where his bones were supposed to lie. Now the present landlady has gone a step further by placing there a tombstone.'

Index